DK

LONDON, NEW YORK,
MELBOURNE, MUNICH, and DELHI

Written and edited by Joe Harris
Designed by Hedi Hunter, Gemma Fletcher,
and Alison Gardner
Maths consultant Sean McArdle
Picture researcher Rob Nunn
Production editor Clare McLean
Production controller Claire Pearson
Jacket editor Mariza O'Keeffe
Jacket designers Natalie Godwin, Claire
Patane, and Hedi Hunter
Publishing manager Bridget Giles
Art director Rachael Foster
Creative director Jane Bull
Category publisher Mary Ling

First published in Great Britain in 2009 by
Dorling Kindersley Limited
80 Strand, London WC2R 0RL

A CIP catalogue record for this book
is available from the British Library.

ISBN 978-1-40534-136-3

Colour reproduction by Colourscan, Singapore
Printed and bound by Hung Hing, China

Discover more at
www.dk.com

REMEMBER,
REMEMBER

Contents

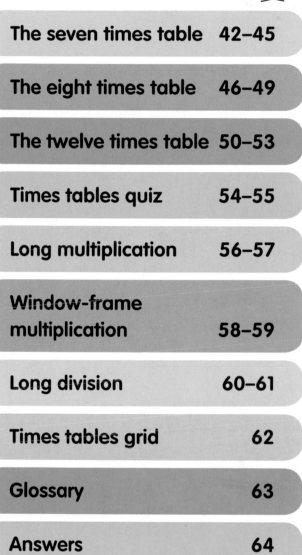

The times tables can be fun!

Learn with games, puzzles, and magic.

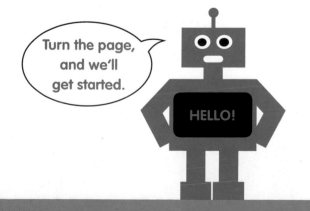

Turn the page, and we'll get started.

HELLO!

Introduction to the times tables

The times tables are special shortcuts that make difficult maths fast and easy.
They do this by telling you the answers to multiplication and division problems.

Multiplication

Multiplication is a fast way of adding up.

How many apples are there on these trees?
There are two ways you could find out.

The slow way: You could add together all the apples like this: **7 + 7 + 7 + 7 = 28**.

The speedy way: Or you could multiply them together, like this: **7 × 4 = 28**.

When you see these words, get ready for multiplication:

times   lots of

groups of

multiply   double

Division

Division is a fast way of subtracting until you approach or reach zero.

If you pick **15** apples, how many can go in each of these apple pies?
You need to find out how many lots of five are the same as **15**.

When you see these words, get ready for division:

share   between

divide

equal groups   into

The slow way: You could find out by subtracting, like this: **15 - 5 - 5 - 5 = 0**.
That shows that **3** lots of **5** are the same as **15**, so **3** apples can go in each pie.

The speedy way: Or you could divide them together, like this: **15 ÷ 5 = 3**.

When do we use the times tables?

We use the times tables constantly in our everyday lives.

3 eggs × 3 = 9 eggs.

When we're cooking.

2 pounds × 3 = 6 pounds.

When we're shopping.

10 slices ÷ 5 = 2 slices each.

When we're sharing.

We use the times tables all the time – sometimes without knowing it!

2 points × 6 = 12 points.

When we're playing sports.

5 minutes × 5 = 25 minutes past.

When we're telling the time.

Learning with songs

It's easy to remember words when they're put to a tune. To help you learn your times tables, we've put together some songs that you can download from the Dorling Kindersley website.

The songs repeat each times table five times. Try to join in with singing the times tables as soon as you can. You can play a game by trying to call out the answers before they're sung. If you like, you can dance to the music too!

To download the songs, go online to this internet address: www.dk.com/timestables.

1x

Here's the 1 times table:

$1 \times 1 = 1$

$2 \times 1 = 2$

$3 \times 1 = 3$

$4 \times 1 = 4$

$5 \times 1 = 5$

$6 \times 1 = 6$

$7 \times 1 = 7$

$8 \times 1 = 8$

$9 \times 1 = 9$

$10 \times 1 = 10$

$11 \times 1 = 11$

$12 \times 1 = 12$

Read the answers to the one times table. You will be counting from **1** to **12**.

The one times table

When you multiply by one, the answer is the same as the number you started with. Nothing changes.

Just one lot of...

Multiplying by one means the same as having one lot of something.

For example, **1** bag of **7** marbles. How many marbles? **7**.

1 bag of 7 marbles

How many?

1 net of **3** fish. How many fish?

1 flower with **6** petals. How many petals?

1 basket with **12** apples. How many apples?

1 purse with **7** coins. How many coins?

The one times mirror

Multiplying a number by **1** is like putting it in front of the mirror. You see the same thing again.

So, $8 \times 1 = 8$.

8 8

The zero times table

When you multiply by zero, you're saying that there are zero lots of something. In other words, nothing at all.

Nothing at all

If you know that something is empty, it doesn't matter how many lots of it you have.

For example: **1** sweets jar with **0** sweets. How many sweets? **0**.

1 jar with 0 sweets

2 birdcages with **0** birds. How many birds?

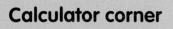

3 ponds with **0** frogs. How many frogs?

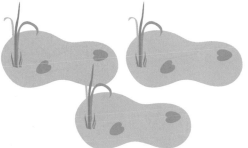

4 baskets with **0** eggs. How many eggs?

Calculator corner

1,000,000

Type 1,000,000 into your calculator, then press "× 0 =". What is the answer? This shows that it doesn't matter how big a number is – multiplying by zero still makes zero.

The ferocious number eater

The number **0** is like a ravenous monster. If you put any other number in a multiplication with **0**, the **0** will eat it up.

0×

Here's the 0 times table:

1 × 0 = 0
2 × 0 = 0
3 × 0 = 0
4 × 0 = 0
5 × 0 = 0
6 × 0 = 0
7 × 0 = 0
8 × 0 = 0
9 × 0 = 0
10 × 0 = 0
11 × 0 = 0
12 × 0 = 0

Answers: 0 birds, 0 frogs, 0 eggs.

2×

Here's the 2 times table:

$1 \times 2 = 2$

$2 \times 2 = 4$

$3 \times 2 = 6$

$4 \times 2 = 8$

$5 \times 2 = 10$

$6 \times 2 = 12$

$7 \times 2 = 14$

$8 \times 2 = 16$

$9 \times 2 = 18$

$10 \times 2 = 20$

$11 \times 2 = 22$

$12 \times 2 = 24$

Notice that every answer to the **2×** table is an **even number**.

The two times table

The two times table is all about doubling, halving, and pairs. It's quick to learn, and easy to use.

Counting in pairs

Many everyday things come in pairs. You can count them faster by counting in twos, like this: **2, 4, 6, 8, 10, 12, 14, 16, 18, 20, 22, 24.**

A pair of shoes   **A pair of socks**   **A pair of gloves**

Count these in groups of two

How many shoes in **3** pairs?

The answer is **6**.

How many socks in **5** pairs?

How many gloves in **6** pairs?

Answers: 10 socks, 12 gloves.

Counting pairs is a kind of multiplication. Instead of writing "Four pairs are eight," you can write that "**4 x 2 = 8**." This is because a pair is a group of two.

4 × 2 = 8

Odd and even numbers

Even numbers end in

2 4 6 8 0

Odd numbers end in

1 3 5 7 9

All the answers in the **2x** table end in an even number. This pattern will help you to remember them.

Can you tell whether these numbers are odd or even?

52

436

452,789

1	2	3	4	5	6	7	8	9	10	11	12
odd	even	odd	even	odd	even	odd	even	odd	even	odd	even

Doubling machine

You can think of the **2x** table as an incredible doubling machine. Whatever you put in, twice as much comes out! Wouldn't it be handy to have a machine like that?

1 sock, 1 teddy bear, 2 footballs and 4 coins go in.

REMEMBER, REMEMBER

Read out loud all the questions and answers in the **2x** table. Then use your hand or a bookmark to cover up the answers, and try saying them again. Can you get them all right?

IN

DOUBLING MACHINE

How many footballs are there?

How many coins come out?

How many teddy bears are there?

How many socks come out?

OUT

Answers: 52 is even, 436 is even, 452,789 is odd. 4 footballs, 8 coins, 2 teddy bears, 2 socks.

9

2×

Let's go shopping

The **2×** table can help you to work out how much things cost. This will be very helpful when you go to the shops!

Two times toffees

Each of these toffees costs **2 pence**.

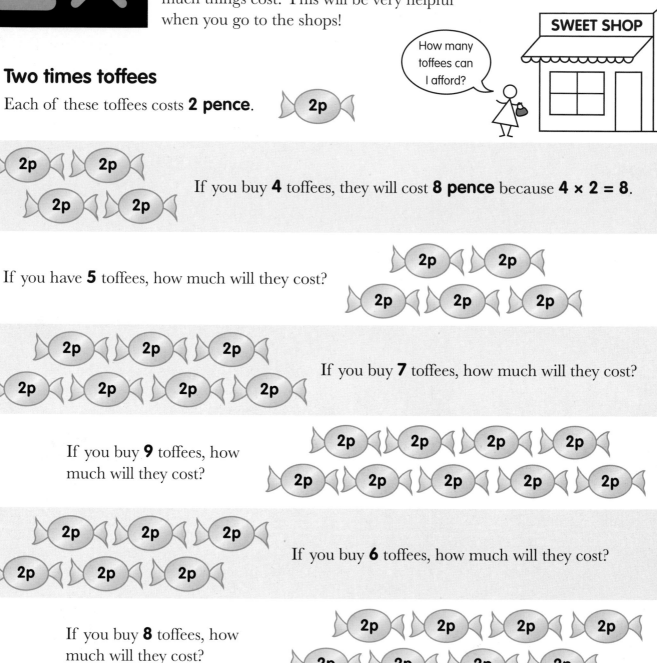

If you buy **4** toffees, they will cost **8 pence** because **4 × 2 = 8**.

If you have **5** toffees, how much will they cost?

If you buy **7** toffees, how much will they cost?

If you buy **9** toffees, how much will they cost?

If you buy **6** toffees, how much will they cost?

If you buy **8** toffees, how much will they cost?

If you buy **11** toffees, how much will they cost?

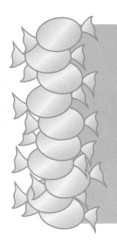

Be fair – share!

Imagine you and a friend are sharing out **24** toffees between you. How many toffees will you each have?

How many toffees × 2 = 24?

This is a bit trickier.

Calculator corner

$$2 \times 2 =$$

What do you think $2 \times 2 \times 2 \times 2$ equals? Try typing it into your calculator. How large a number do you think you will get if you type 2, then "× 2 =" 20 times? Get ready for a surprise.

Paperboy

You can think of the **2×** table as a number line. This boy is delivering newspapers. He drops them off at every other house. The houses that he stops at are the same as the answers to the two times table. Where will he stop next?

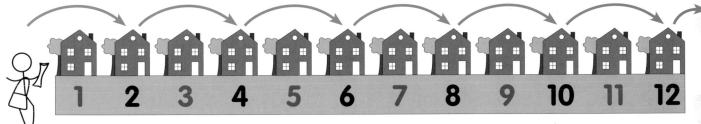

1 2 3 4 5 6 7 8 9 10 11 12

The word "multiple" comes from "multiplication". 6 is a multiple of 2, because 2 can be multiplied by another number (3) to make 6.

Odd ones out

Which of these numbers are not multiples of **2**? (Remember that all the answers in the **2×** table are even numbers.)

24 7 14 6 15 9 21 13 8 10

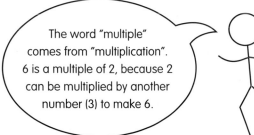

TOP TIP

If you know how to add, the **2×** table is easy. Just remember that two times a number means the same as adding that number to itself.

5 × 2 is the same as **5 + 5**.

Answers: 12 toffees × 2=24. The paperboy will stop at number 14 next. 7, 15, 9, 13, and 21 are not multiples of two.

11

The five times table

All that you need to count in fives are your hands. And if you can count in fives, then you can multiply by five too!

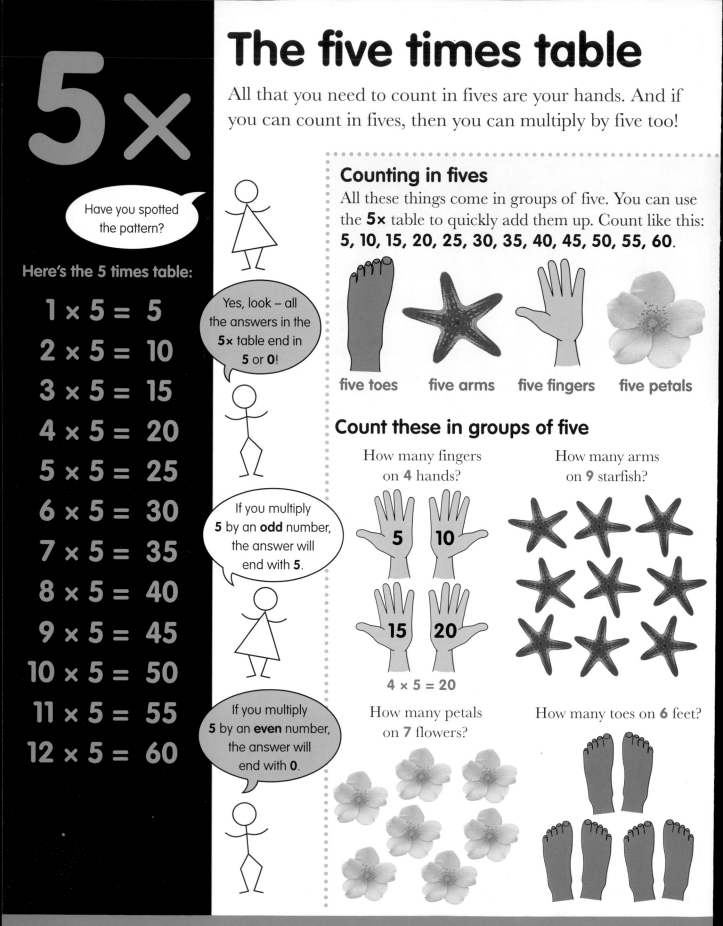

5×

Have you spotted the pattern?

Here's the 5 times table:

$1 \times 5 = 5$

$2 \times 5 = 10$

$3 \times 5 = 15$

$4 \times 5 = 20$

$5 \times 5 = 25$

$6 \times 5 = 30$

$7 \times 5 = 35$

$8 \times 5 = 40$

$9 \times 5 = 45$

$10 \times 5 = 50$

$11 \times 5 = 55$

$12 \times 5 = 60$

Yes, look – all the answers in the **5×** table end in **5** or **0**!

If you multiply **5** by an **odd** number, the answer will end with **5**.

If you multiply **5** by an **even** number, the answer will end with **0**.

Counting in fives

All these things come in groups of five. You can use the **5×** table to quickly add them up. Count like this:
5, 10, 15, 20, 25, 30, 35, 40, 45, 50, 55, 60.

five toes   five arms   five fingers   five petals

Count these in groups of five

How many fingers on **4** hands?

5 **10** **15** **20**

$4 \times 5 = 20$

How many arms on **9** starfish?

How many petals on **7** flowers?

How many toes on **6** feet?

Practice makes perfect

Read the questions and answers in the **5×** table out loud. Then give this book to a friend, and ask them to test you. Can you remember the answers?

Backwards and forwards

Have you noticed that the answer to **2 × 5** is the same as the answer to **5 × 2**?

$$5 × 2 = 10$$
$$2 × 5 = 10$$

Five **2-pence** toffees cost exactly the same as two **5-pence** lollipops.

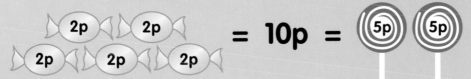

Multiplications give the same answer whichever way round you put the numbers. This means that you already know some of the answers to the other times tables.

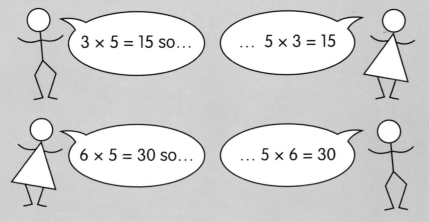

3 × 5 = 15 so...   ... 5 × 3 = 15

6 × 5 = 30 so...   ... 5 × 6 = 30

Don't look down!

Cleaning windows

You can also think of the **5×** table as a number line. Imagine a window cleaner who stops at every fifth floor of a skyscraper. Where will he stop next?

5×

Five times clock

The **5×** table helps you to tell the time. There are **5** minutes between each number on the clock face.

If the minute hand of a clock points to **2**, that means it's **10** minutes past because **5 × 2 = 10**.

If the minute hand of a clock points to **5**, that means it's **25** minutes past because **5 × 5 = 25**.

How many minutes past the hour is it when the minute hand points to **6**?

How many minutes past the hour is it when the minute hand points to **9**?

Rows and columns

You can use the times tables to count objects in rows and columns. First count how many columns there are, then count how many rows. Multiply those numbers together.

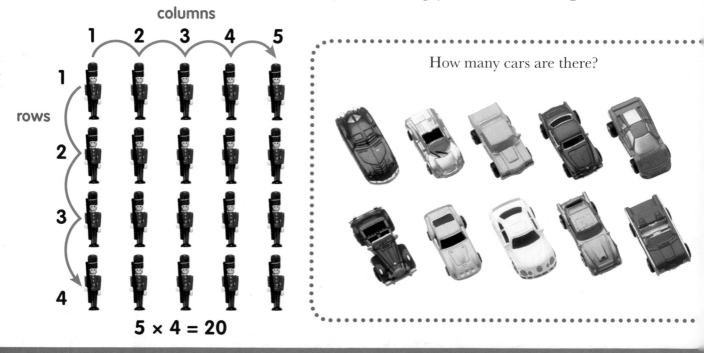

columns

1 2 3 4 5

rows

1

2

3

4

5 × 4 = 20

How many cars are there?

Answers: 30 minutes past, 45 minutes past.

Let's go shopping again

Each of these coins is worth **5** pence.

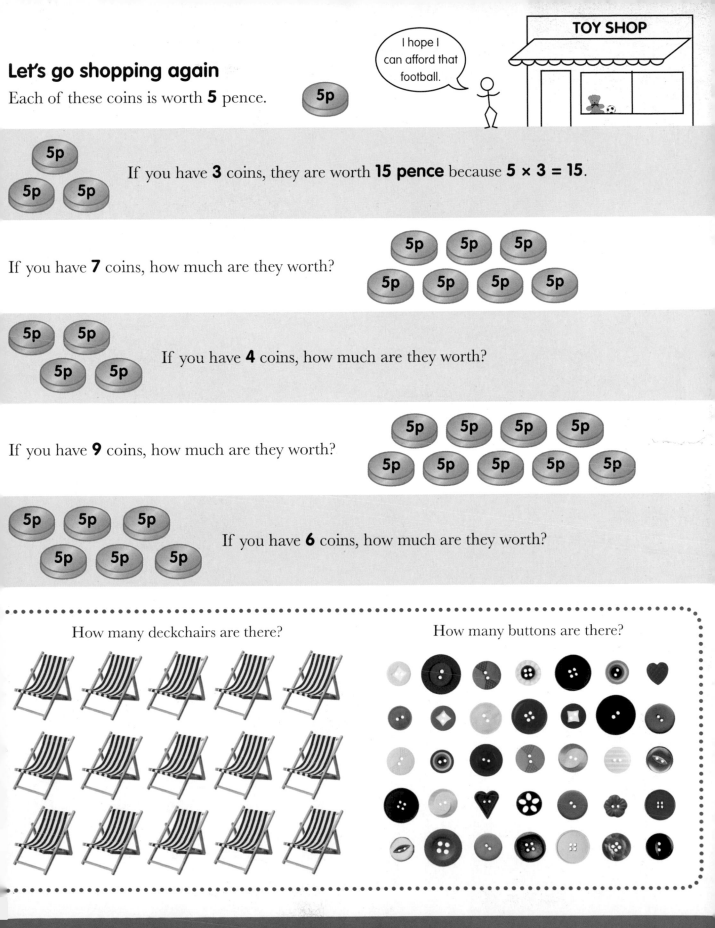

5p

I hope I can afford that football.

TOY SHOP

If you have **3** coins, they are worth **15 pence** because **5 × 3 = 15**.

If you have **7** coins, how much are they worth?

If you have **4** coins, how much are they worth?

If you have **9** coins, how much are they worth?

If you have **6** coins, how much are they worth?

How many deckchairs are there?

How many buttons are there?

Answers: 10 cars, 15 deckchairs, 35 buttons, 35p, 20p, 45p, 30p.

15

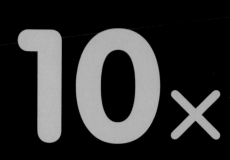

10×

The ten times table

You don't need to memorize this times table. All you need to learn is the simple pattern in the numbers.

Here's the 10 times table:

1 × 10 = 10

2 × 10 = 20

3 × 10 = 30

4 × 10 = 40

5 × 10 = 50

6 × 10 = 60

7 × 10 = 70

8 × 10 = 80

9 × 10 = 90

10 × 10 = 100

11 × 10 = 110

12 × 10 = 120

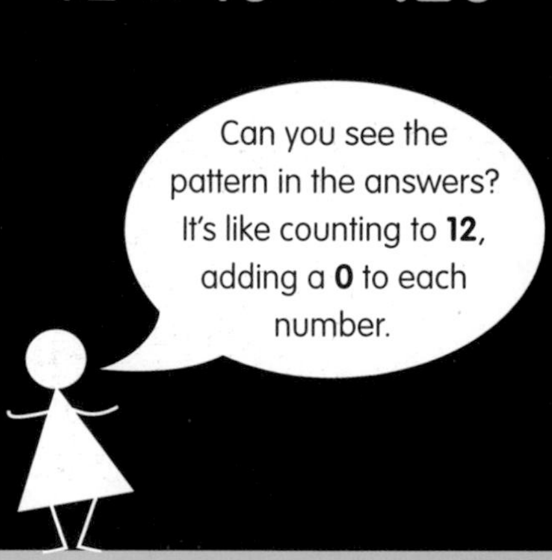
Can you see the pattern in the answers? It's like counting to **12**, adding a **0** to each number.

Just add zero

To make a number ten times larger, you add a zero to the end. This means that the units in the number become tens, and if there are any tens they become hundreds.

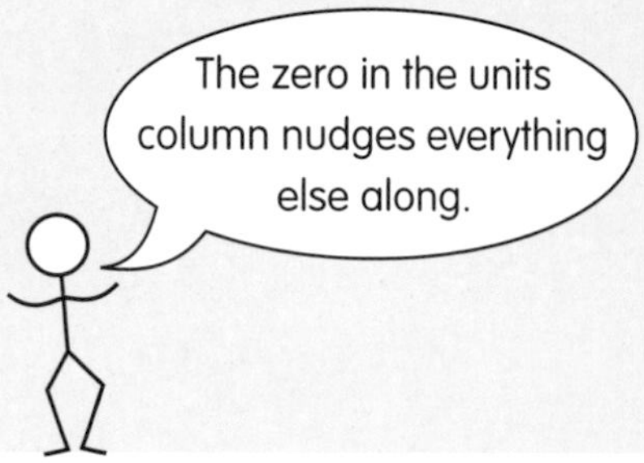
The zero in the units column nudges everything else along.

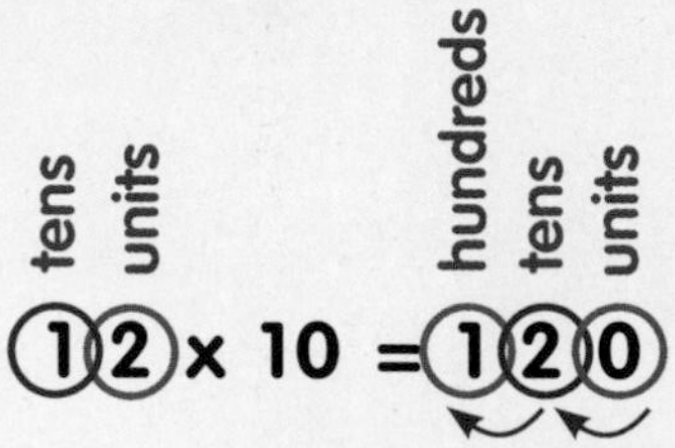
tens
units
hundreds
tens
units
12 × 10 = 120

There are **10** pencils in each group. How many altogether?

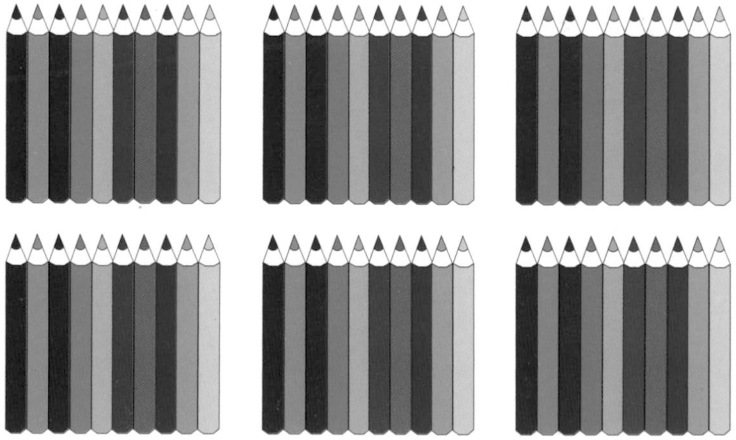

How many paperclips in these four groups of **10**?

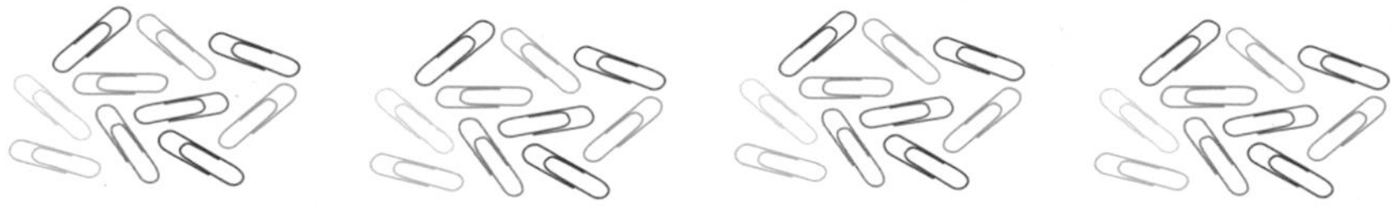

Now try multiplying these large numbers by **10**.

73 × 10 =

135 × 10 =

245 × 10 =

Can you work out what **451,236** multiplied by ten equals?

Answers: 60 pencils, 40 paperclips. 73 × 10 = 730. 135 × 10 = 1,350. 245 × 10 = 2,450. 451,236 × 10 = 4,512,360.

Let's go bowling

For each pin that you knock over, you score **10** points. Can you tell how many points you would score in each of these examples?

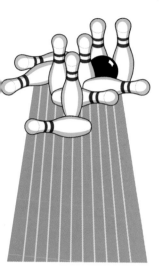

Hundreds and thousands

It's just as easy to multiply by **100** or **1,000**. To multiply a whole number by **100**, add two zeros to the end. To multiply a whole number by **1,000**, add three zeros. Make sure you add the same number of zeros to the answer as there are in the multiplier.

In this game, you score points for each alien invader that you disintegrate. Can you work out how many points have been scored in each example?

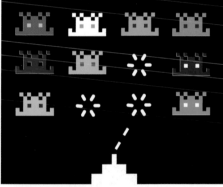

Each alien is worth 100 points.

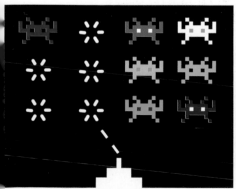

Each alien is worth 1,000 points.

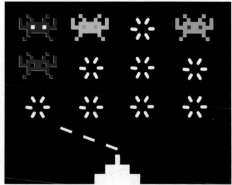

Each alien is worth 1,000 points.

The final countdown

It's easy to count down from **10** to **1**. But how quickly can you count down in tens?

100

90

80

70

60

50

40

30

20

10

Blast off!

Answers: Bowling – 50 points, 60 points, 80 points. Invaders – 300 points, 5,000 points, 8,000 points.

17

10×

TOP TIP

To multiply by numbers ending with a **0**, break the problem into two steps.

Imagine you want to multiply 50 by 6.

STEP 1 Multiply by the first part of the number, ignoring the zero.

$$5\cancel{0} \times 6 = 30$$

STEP 2 Now multiply by **10**.

$$30 \times \boxed{10} = 300$$

Give me ten!
multiplication game

This fast-paced two-player game will help you practise your times tables up to **10 × 10**.

Each player must think of a number between **0** and **10** in their head. They both hold out their hands and call out, "Ready, steady, go!" then hold up that number of fingers.

Now each player tries to work out the answer to the number of fingers held up on their hands, multiplied by the number of fingers held up on the other player's hands.

Whoever calls out the correct answer first wins a point. Keep playing until one player has won ten points.

Hey big spender

To multiply money by **10**, move the decimal point along to the right and add a zero at the end of the pence column. So for example:

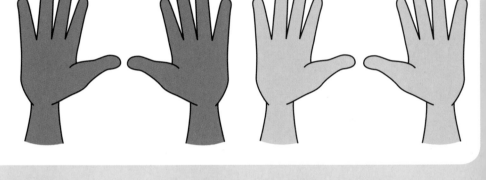

£8.50 × 10 = £85.00

Make a times tables slider

This simple make-and-do project will turn times tables practice into a fun quiz game.

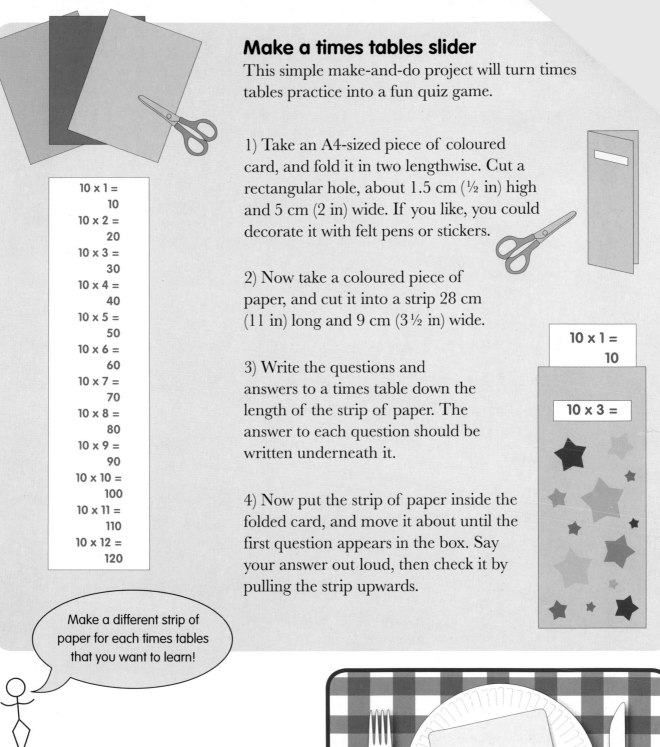

1) Take an A4-sized piece of coloured card, and fold it in two lengthwise. Cut a rectangular hole, about 1.5 cm (½ in) high and 5 cm (2 in) wide. If you like, you could decorate it with felt pens or stickers.

2) Now take a coloured piece of paper, and cut it into a strip 28 cm (11 in) long and 9 cm (3 ½ in) wide.

3) Write the questions and answers to a times table down the length of the strip of paper. The answer to each question should be written underneath it.

4) Now put the strip of paper inside the folded card, and move it about until the first question appears in the box. Say your answer out loud, then check it by pulling the strip upwards.

10 x 1 =
10
10 x 2 =
20
10 x 3 =
30
10 x 4 =
40
10 x 5 =
50
10 x 6 =
60
10 x 7 =
70
10 x 8 =
80
10 x 9 =
90
10 x 10 =
100
10 x 11 =
110
10 x 12 =
120

10 x 1 =
10

10 x 3 =

Make a different strip of paper for each times tables that you want to learn!

Picnic puzzler

If forks come in packs of **6**, and knives come in packs of **10**, how many packs of forks and how many packs of knives would you need to buy in order to have the same number of each?

Answer: You would need 5 packs of forks and 3 packs of knives.

19

The four times table

If you already know the two times table well, you won't find it hard to learn the four times table. Remember to look for the patterns in the answers.

Have you spotted the patterns?

Here's the 4 times table:

1 × 4 = 4
2 × 4 = 8
3 × 4 = 12
4 × 4 = 16
5 × 4 = 20
6 × 4 = 24
7 × 4 = 28
8 × 4 = 32
9 × 4 = 36
10 × 4 = 40
11 × 4 = 44
12 × 4 = 48

Yes, look – all the answers in the four times tables are **EVEN** numbers.

There's another pattern too… As you read down the table the answers end **4, 8, 2, 6, 0**, over and over.

Counting in fours

Many everyday objects come in groups of four. You can use the four times table to count them.

A car has 4 wheels

A chair has 4 legs

A dog has 4 legs

Count these in groups of four

How many wheels on **8** cars?

How many legs on **4** chairs?

8 × 4 = 32

How many legs on **6** dogs?

First divide the number in half.
(This is the same as dividing by **2**.)

Then divide it in half again.

8 cakes

4 cakes

4 cakes

½

8 cakes

½

4 cakes

4 cakes

Calculator corner

44,444

Type these sums into a calculator,
and write the answers down.

4 x 4 =
44 x 4 =
444 x 4 =
4444 x 4 =
44444 x 4 =

You can keep going if you like.
Can you spot the surprising
pattern in your answers?

TOP TIP

If you multiply two **even** numbers
together, you get an **even** answer.
Multiply two **odd** numbers together,
and you get an **odd** answer. An **odd**
number times an **even** number
gives an **even** answer.

EVEN x EVEN = EVEN

ODD x ODD = ODD

ODD x EVEN = EVEN

Piggy banks

Divide the money in these piggy
banks between **4** children. How
much will they each receive?

36p

16p

48p

24p

16 ÷ 4 = 4

Answers: 36p shared between 4 is 9p each. 48p shared between 4 is 12p each. 24p shared between 4 is 6p each.

23

11×

Here's the 11 times table:

$1 \times 11 = 11$

$2 \times 11 = 22$

$3 \times 11 = 33$

$4 \times 11 = 44$

$5 \times 11 = 55$

$6 \times 11 = 66$

$7 \times 11 = 77$

$8 \times 11 = 88$

$9 \times 11 = 99$

$10 \times 11 = 110$

$11 \times 11 = 121$

$12 \times 11 = 132$

The eleven times table

A helpful pattern

There is a simple way of multiplying single-digit numbers by **11**. Imagine you're multiplying **3** by **11**. Just think of the same number again, written next to it: **33**.

Another pattern

There is another pattern that will help you remember the three-digit answers for **10 × 11**, **11 × 11**, and **12 × 11**. It also works with other problems up to **18 × 11**.

The first and last digits in the answer to **10 × 11** are **1** and **0**.

Add the first and last numbers of the answer together to get the middle number: **1 + 0 = 1**.

$$10 \times 11 = 1\ 0$$
$$10 \times 11 = 110$$

$$12 \times 11 = 1\ 2$$
$$12 \times 11 = 132$$

The first and the last number in the answer to **12 × 11** are **1** and **2**.

Add the first and last numbers of the answer together to get the middle number: **1 + 2 = 3**.

Let's go fly a kite

Can you work out the answers to **10 × 11** to **18 × 11**? Follow the strings to see whether you're right.

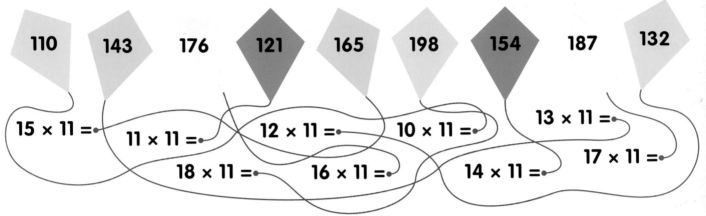

110 143 176 121 165 198 154 187 132

15 × 11 =

11 × 11 =

12 × 11 =

10 × 11 =

13 × 11 =

18 × 11 =

16 × 11 =

14 × 11 =

17 × 11 =

Football tournament

Footballers play in teams of **11** players.

How many players in **2** teams?

How many players in **6** teams?

How many players in **7** teams?

How many players in **12** teams?

Answer: 22 players in 2 teams, 66 players in 6 teams, 77 players in 7 teams, and 132 players in 12 teams.

25

11×

Halftime drinks and snacks

You're buying the halftime refreshments for your local football team. There are **11** people on the team. How much will it cost you to buy enough of these for the whole team? Remember that **100p** is **£1**.

40p **70p** **50p** **40p** **80p**

Invisible number 11 trick

This magic trick will amaze your friends.

1. Dip a paintbrush in lemon juice and write the number **11** on a piece of paper. When the juice dries, the answer will be invisible. Show this blank paper to your audience.

2. Ask a volunteer to secretly think of a three-digit number.

465

3. Ask them to type the number into a calculator twice. If the number they thought of was **465**, they should type:

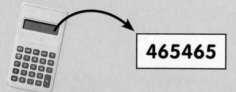

465465

4. First tell them to divide that number by lucky number **7**.

465,465 ÷ 7 = 66,495

5. Now tell them to divide it by the least lucky number: **13**.

66,495 ÷ 13 = 5,115

6. Finally, tell them to divide by the number they first thought of.

5,115 ÷ 465 = 11

7. Tell your audience that you are going to magically write the answer on the blank paper. Hold the paper near a hot lightbulb, and the number **11** will magically appear!

Ta-dah!

Wow!

11

Times tables pairs game

This two-player game will help you learn your times tables, at the same time as improving your memory.

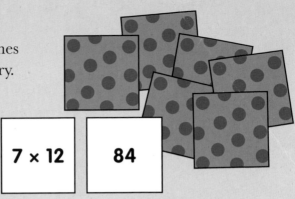

1. First, you'll need to cut out **24** pieces of card. Choose **12** sums you find difficult, and write the questions on half of the cards, and the answers on the other half. Leave one side of each card blank.

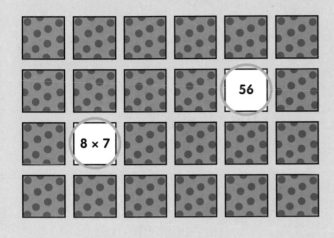

2. Shuffle the cards together, and spread them out face-down on the table in rows and columns, without looking at them.

3. Each player takes it in turns to turn over two cards. If the two cards they turn over are a matching pair showing a question and the correct answer, then they keep them. Otherwise they turn them face down again.

4. When there are no cards left, the winner is whoever has the most cards.

> Watch the cards your opponent turns over, and try to remember them for your turn.

Prime time

The number **11** is a prime number. This means that it is only divisible by two natural numbers: **1** and itself. The number **1** is not a prime number. These are also prime numbers:

2   **3**   **5**   **7**

Can you work out which is the next prime number after **11**?

TOP TIP

If you ever have any problems multiplying large numbers by **11**, just remember: multiply by **10**, then add the original number.

Calculator corner

$11 \times 11 =$

Type these equations into your calculator, and an interesting pattern will appear.

$11 \times 11 =$
$111 \times 111 =$
$1,111 \times 1,111 =$
$1,1111 \times 1,1111 =$

Can you guess what the next number in the pattern will be?

$11,111 \times 11,111 = ?$

3×

$1 \times 3 = 3$

$2 \times 3 = 6$

$3 \times 3 = 9$

$4 \times 3 = 12$

$5 \times 3 = 15$

$6 \times 3 = 18$

$7 \times 3 = 21$

$8 \times 3 = 24$

$9 \times 3 = 27$

$10 \times 3 = 30$

$11 \times 3 = 33$

$12 \times 3 = 36$

Don't forget: if you multiply **3** by an **odd** number, the answer will be an **odd** number.

But if you multiply **3** by an **even** number, the answer is an **even** number.

The three times table

There is no sneaky shortcut to learning the three times table – this one takes practice. But once you have mastered it, you will have learnt most of your times tables.

Counting in threes

Many objects with three parts start with "tri" – like triangles, tricycles and triplets. Can you count in threes?

A triangle has 3 sides   **A tricycle has 3 wheels**   **A triplet has 3 notes**

Count these in groups of three

How many wheels on **4** tricycles?

$4 \times 3 = 12$

How many sides on **7** triangles?

How many notes in **9** triplets?

Carrot patch number line

You can also look at the **3** times table as a number line. Look at this rabbit – each time she jumps, she skips over two carrots and takes a nibble at the third. Try closing your eyes and saying out loud where she will land each time. Can you bounce right up to carrot number **36**?

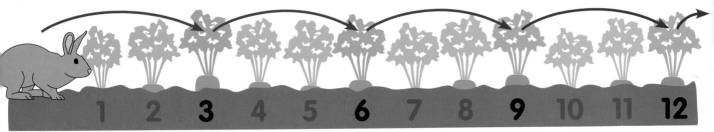

Rows and columns

How many balls are there of each colour? Find out by multiplying the rows and columns together. You could check your answers by counting the marbles.

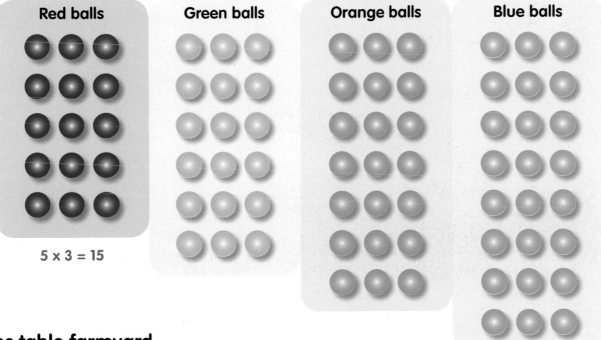

Red balls   **Green balls**   **Orange balls**   **Blue balls**

5 × 3 = 15

Times table farmyard

This is a noisy game for two or more players. Take it in turns to call out numbers, counting from **1**. Whenever someone reaches a multiple of three (an answer in the **3×** table), they have to make an animal noise.

1   2   Woof!   4   5   Baa!   7

3×

Bon appetit!

Most people eat **3** meals each day.

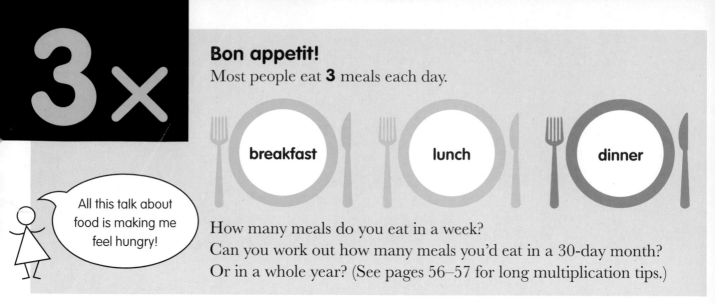

breakfast   lunch   dinner

All this talk about food is making me feel hungry!

How many meals do you eat in a week?
Can you work out how many meals you'd eat in a 30-day month?
Or in a whole year? (See pages 56–57 for long multiplication tips.)

Minesweeper

Can you find a safe route through this minefield? Start where it says "**go**" and move across, up, or down until you reach "**end**". But you must avoid the mines! Any square with a multiple of three has a mine under it.

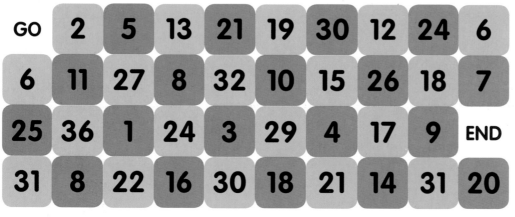

GO

2	5	13	21	19	30	12	24	6
6	11	27	8	32	10	15	26	18	7
25	36	1	24	3	29	4	17	9	END
31	8	22	16	30	18	21	14	31	20

The solution is on page 64.

It all adds up

The first three answers in the **3×** table are **3**, **6**, and **9**. If you add together the digits of multiples of three, they add up to **3**, **6**, or **9**. You can use this as a way of checking your answers.

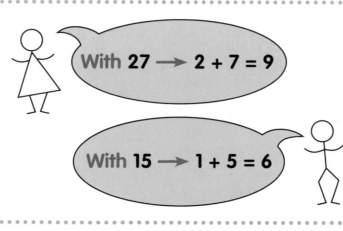

With 27 → 2 + 7 = 9

With 15 → 1 + 5 = 6

Answers: 21 meals in a week. 90 meals in a 30-day month. 1,095 meals in a non-leap year.

Magic number 3 card trick

Here's another magic trick you can perform for a friend. You'll need a deck of cards and a calculator.

I chose number 8.

1. Ask your friend to secretly choose a card from the pack. It has to be a number card, not a face card like a jack, king, or queen. Tell your friend to remember their card, and place it face-down on the table.

I chose number 3.

2. Now secretly choose your own card, and place this face-down on the table too. For the trick to work, you have to choose a **3**.

3. Once your friend has placed their card face-down on the table, give them the calculator. Tell them to enter the number they chose, and do this calculation:

Don't forget to press the = button after each one!

Multiply it by 2
Add 2
Multiply by 5
Subtract 7

$$8 \quad \boxed{\times\ 2\ =} \quad 16$$
$$\boxed{+\ 2\ =} \quad 18$$
$$\boxed{\times\ 5\ =} \quad 90$$
$$\boxed{-\ 7\ =} \quad 83$$

4. Turn over their card, then your card. The numbers on the two cards will match the numbers on the calculator screen!

Our numbers match the answer!

8   3

This technique also works with bigger numbers. If you add together the digits of the answer and get a two- or three-digit number, then you will need to add those digits together as well.

With 267 ⟶ 2 + 6 + 7 = 15
and 1 + 5 = 6
So **267** is a multiple of **3**.

With 846 ⟶ 8 + 4 + 6 = 18
and 1 + 8 = 9
So **846** is a multiple of **3**.

Is **348** a multiple of **3**?

What about **255**?

How well do you know your time tables so far?

You can use this quiz to test yourself on the times tables you've learnt up to now. If you get stuck on some problems, make sure you review those tables later. The answers are on page 64.

Talking times tables

There are many ways of talking about the times tables. Can you answer each question?

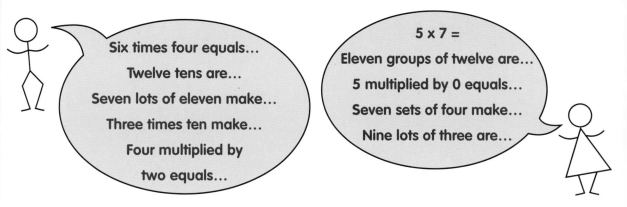

Six times four equals…

Twelve tens are…

Seven lots of eleven make…

Three times ten make…

Four multiplied by two equals…

5 x 7 =

Eleven groups of twelve are…

5 multiplied by 0 equals…

Seven sets of four make…

Nine lots of three are…

How many wheels?

11 bicycles   4 tricycles   5 trucks   12 cars   6 motorbikes

Big city buildings

How many windows are there on each of these buildings?

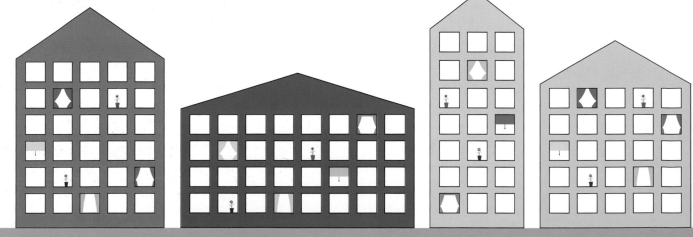

Fruit salad

You're making a fruit salad. How much will it cost you to buy…

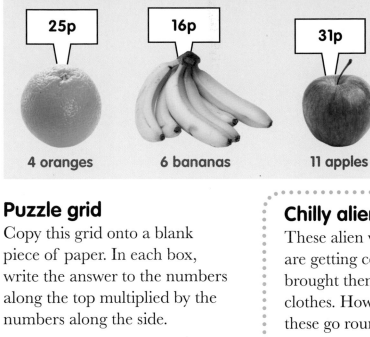

25p — 4 oranges

16p — 6 bananas

31p — 11 apples

82p — 1 watermelon

63p — 2 pineapples

Puzzle grid

Copy this grid onto a blank piece of paper. In each box, write the answer to the numbers along the top multiplied by the numbers along the side.

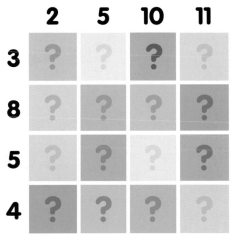

	2	5	10	11
3	?	?	?	?
8	?	?	?	?
5	?	?	?	?
4	?	?	?	?

Chilly aliens

These alien visitors to Earth are getting cold, so you've brought them some nice warm clothes. How many aliens will these go round?

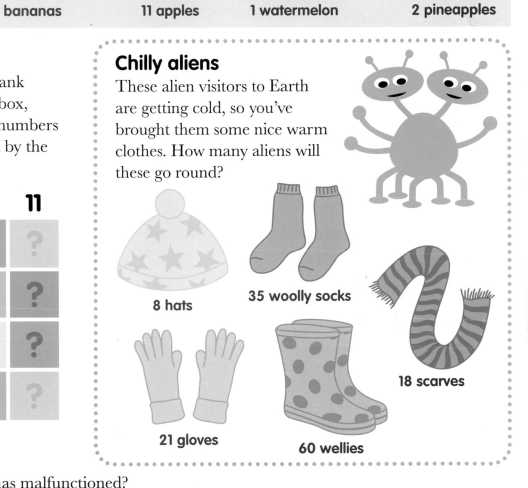

8 hats

35 woolly socks

18 scarves

21 gloves

60 wellies

Error! Error!

Which of these robots has malfunctioned?

9 × 11 = 99

24 ÷ 2 = 12

9 × 4 = 36

24 ÷ 4 = 7

The nine times table

The nine times table may look tricky, but it is one of the easiest tables to learn. There is a simple pattern hidden in the answers.

9×

Have you spotted the pattern?

Here's the 9 times table:

$1 \times 9 = 9$

$2 \times 9 = 18$

$3 \times 9 = 27$

$4 \times 9 = 36$

$5 \times 9 = 45$

$6 \times 9 = 54$

$7 \times 9 = 63$

$8 \times 9 = 72$

$9 \times 9 = 81$

$10 \times 9 = 90$

$11 \times 9 = 99$

$12 \times 9 = 108$

Look: the digits in the units column count down from **9** to **0**.

And between **2 × 9** and **10 × 9**, the tens column counts up from **1** to **9**.

Kitty multiplication

People sometimes say that cats have nine lives. How many lives do the cats below have between them?

1 cat = 9 lives

Count the lives for each group of cats

How many lives for **3** cats?

$3 \times 9 = 27.$

How many lives for **7** cats?

How many lives for **9** cats?

Nine times table number grid

0	1	2	3	4	5	6	7	8	9
10	11	12	13	14	15	16	17	18	19
20	21	22	23	24	25	26	27	28	29
30	31	32	33	34	35	36	37	38	39
40	41	42	43	44	45	46	47	48	49
50	51	52	53	54	55	56	57	58	59
60	61	62	63	64	65	66	67	68	69
70	71	72	73	74	75	76	77	78	79
80	81	82	83	84	85	86	87	88	89
90	91	92	93	94	95	96	97	98	99

> Look what happens if you put the answers to the **9×** table in a grid.

> The answers form a diagonal line!

The nine times table made easy

This is a rule that works for all the answers in the nine times table between **2 × 9** and **10 × 9**. The key is to do some quick mental subtraction.

STEP 1

The answers start with a digit one less than the number you are multiplying by **9**.

STEP 2

The second digit of the answer is equal to **9** minus the first digit.

$2 - 1 = 1$

$$2 × 9 = 18$$

$$2 × 9 = 18$$

$9 - 1 = 8$

$3 - 1 = 2$

$$3 × 9 = 27$$

$$3 × 9 = 27$$

$9 - 2 = 7$

Cats and kittens
If **9** cats each have **9** kittens, how many cats will there be in all?

TOP TIP

Here's an easy way of finding out whether a number is a multiple of nine. You can use this to check your answers. If a number is a multiple of nine, then the digits in the answer will add up to nine.

36 ⟶ $3 + 6 =$ **9**

This works with bigger numbers, too. If you add together the numbers in the answer and get a two-digit number, then you need to add those digits together too.

99 ⟶ $9 + 9 =$ **18**

$1 + 8 =$ **9**

Can you work out whether **783** and **16,947** are multiples of nine?

Answers: 81 kittens and 9 cats gives 90 cats in all. 783 and 16,947 are both multiples of 9.

35

A handy way of multiplying by nine

Here's a way to work out the **9×** table on your hands.

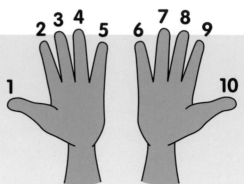

Hold your hands in front of you, palms upwards. Imagine that each of your fingers has a number written on it, from **1** to **10**.

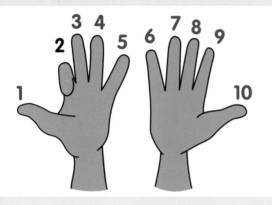

Say you want to multiply **9** by **2**. Start at the left and count along your fingers until you get to the second one. Fold that finger down.

How many fingers are to the left of the finger that's folded down? This is the first digit of your answer. How many fingers are to the right of the finger that's folded down? That's the second digit of your answer.

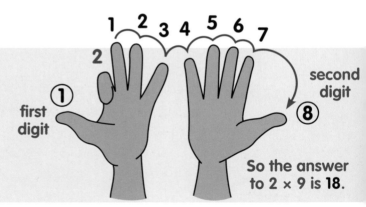

first digit

second digit

So the answer to 2 × 9 is **18**.

Now let's try some more.

What is **6 × 9**?

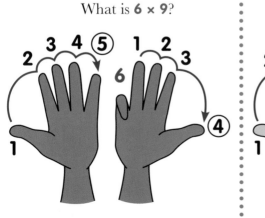

What is **4 × 9**?

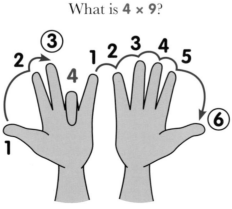

What is **9 × 9**?

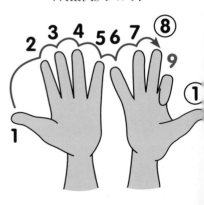

Reversible answers

For each of the answers in the **9×** table, there is another answer with the digits swapped round. For example, **63** is a multiple of nine, but so is **36**, which is **63** reversed. Which multiplications are linked by their reversible answers? Follow the lines to find out. Can you say what the answers are?

2 × 9
(18)

3 × 9

4 × 9

5 × 9

7 × 9

6 × 9

8 × 9

9 × 9
(81)

Nine ti...
Cut out ten ...
and write thes...
on them:

0   1   2

3   4   5

6   7   9   8

Now rearrange them to make **5** answers to equations in the **9** times table.

Incredible number nine magic trick

Write the number **9** on a piece of paper, slip it inside a balloon, and blow the balloon up.

1. Ask a volunteer to pick a three-digit number.

2. Jumble up the three digits in any way to make another number.

3. Take the smaller number away from the larger one.

4. Add the digits in the answer together. If the solution has more than one digit, keep adding the digits together until you have one number.

5. Now tell your audience that you are going to magically write that number on the piece of paper inside the balloon. Pop the balloon, and show them what is written inside. They will be amazed!

943

394

$943 - 394 = 549$

$5 + 4 + 9 = 18$

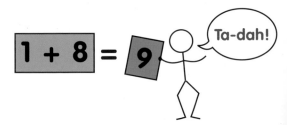

$1 + 8 = 9$

Ta-dah!

Answer to brainteaser: 90, 18 or 81, 27 or 72, 36 or 63, and 45 or 54.

37

The six times table

At this point, you have already learnt nine of the 13 times tables in this book. After you've mastered the six times table, there are only three more to go.

If you multiply **6** by an even number, they both end with the same digit.

Here's the 6 times table:

$1 \times 6 = 6$

$2 \times 6 = 12$

$3 \times 6 = 18$

$4 \times 6 = 24$

$5 \times 6 = 30$

$6 \times 6 = 36$

$7 \times 6 = 42$

$8 \times 6 = 48$

$9 \times 6 = 54$

$10 \times 6 = 60$

$11 \times 6 = 66$

$12 \times 6 = 72$

$8 \times 6 = 4\,\textcircled{8}$

I've spotted something else, too! For the first four of those equations, the first digit is half of the second digit.

$2 \times 6 = \textcircled{1}\,2$

$6 \times 6 = \textcircled{3}\,6$

Counting in sixes

Many groceries come in groups of six. You can count them using the six times table.

A string of 6 sausages

A box of 6 eggs

Yoghurts come in packs of 6

Count these in groups of six

If you have **2** strings of **6** sausages, how many sausages do you have?

If you have **8** boxes of **6** eggs, how many eggs do you have?

$2 \times 6 = 12$

How many yoghurts are here?
Count the rows and columns.

Taking the plunge

By multiplying the length of a rectangle by its width, you can find its area. Each of these swimming pools is **6** metres wide, but they each have a different length. Can you find their areas in metres squared?

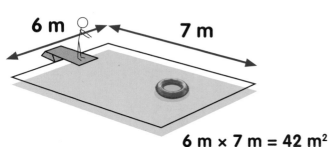

6 m · 7 m

$$6 \text{ m} \times 7 \text{ m} = 42 \text{ m}^2$$

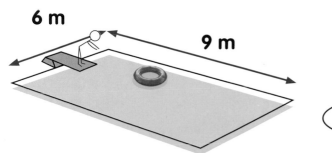

6 m · 9 m

6 m · 11 m

Did you get them all right?

Dotty dominoes game

This two-player game will help you practise your times tables up to **6×**. Place some dominoes face down on a table, and mix them up. Take it in turns to turn one over. When it's your turn, you must multiply the two sides of the domino together and say the answer out loud. If you get it right, you can keep the domino. If you're wrong, turn it back over.

$1 \times 3 = \mathbf{3}$

$5 \times 3 = \mathbf{15}$

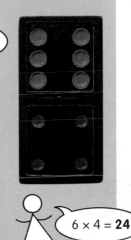

$6 \times 4 = \mathbf{24}$

Whoever has the most dominoes at the end of the game wins.

TOP TIP

If you get stuck with the **6x** table, remember that it's the same as the **3x** table **doubled**.

7 × 6 is the same as

7 × 3, twice.

Or you can take the **5x** table as a starting point, and add **1** more set.

4 × 6 is the same as

4 × 5, + another 4.

6×

How bee-wildering

These multiplications from the **6×** table have got all mixed up. Can you work out what they should say?

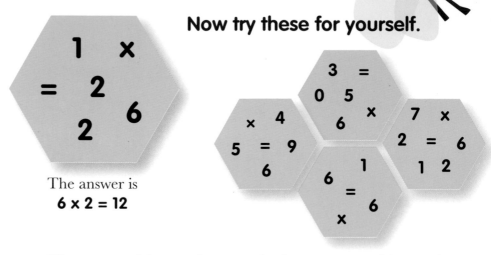

1 ×
= 2
2 6

The answer is
6 × 2 = 12

Now try these for yourself.

3 =
0 5 ×
× 4 6
5 = 9
6 1
6 =
6
×

7 ×
2 = 6
1 2

How many sides are there on the hexagons on this page?

Sandcastles

You have built **6** sandcastles, and want to divide the decorations you have equally between them. How many of each decoration will you put on each castle?

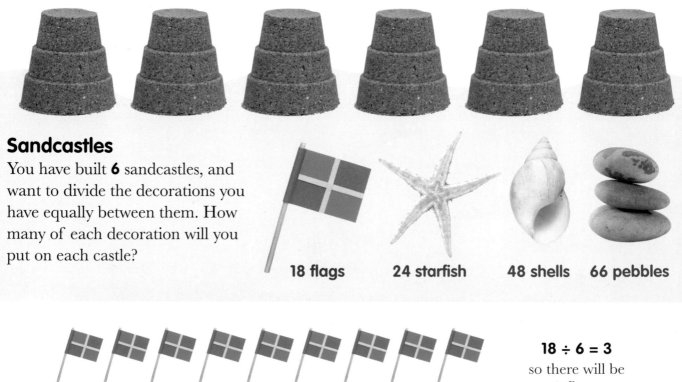

18 flags   **24 starfish**   **48 shells**   **66 pebbles**

18 ÷ 6 = 3
so there will be
3 flags
on each sandcastle

The finger calculator

Here's a brilliant way of multiplying together numbers between **6** and **9**, using only your All you need to know to do this are the **1** to **4** times tables. This technique will help you your answers for some of the trickiest multiplication problems.

Imagine you want to multiply together **8** and **6**.
8 × 6 = ?

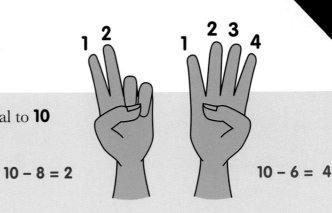

Hold up a number of fingers on each hand equal to **10** minus the numbers you are multiplying.

10 − 8 = 2   **10 − 6 = 4**

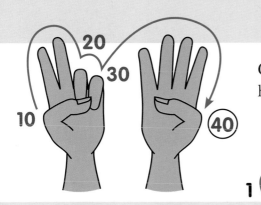

Count the bent fingers on both hands, and multiply by **10**.

4 × 10 = (**40**)

Count the straight fingers on each hand, and multiply them together.

2 × 4 is (**8.**)

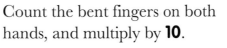

Add the two resulting numbers together.

Bent fingers **= 40**
and straight fingers **= 8**
So the answer is **40 + 8 = 48**

Now try these for yourself.

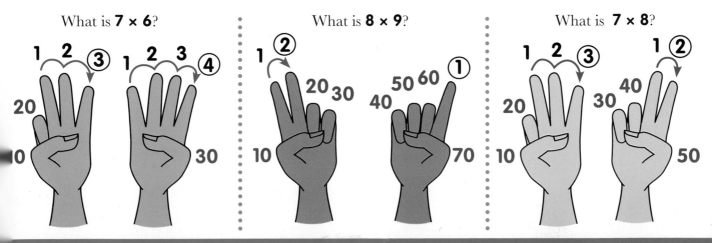

What is **7 × 6**?

What is **8 × 9**?

What is **7 × 8**?

The seven times table

The seven times table is one of the hardest to learn from scratch. But if you've learnt all the previous times tables in this book, then you'll already know most of the sevens.

your fingers.
to check

Here's the 7 times table:

$1 \times 7 = 7$

$2 \times 7 = 14$

$3 \times 7 = 21$

$4 \times 7 = 28$

$5 \times 7 = 35$

$6 \times 7 = 42$

$7 \times 7 = 49$

$8 \times 7 = 56$

$9 \times 7 = 63$

$10 \times 7 = 70$

$11 \times 7 = 77$

$12 \times 7 = 84$

There are only **3** new multiplications that you haven't already learnt in the **7×** table.

$7 \times 7 = 49$
$7 \times 8 = 56$
$8 \times 7 = 56$
$8 \times 8 = 64$
$7 \times 12 = 84$
$12 \times 7 = 84$
$8 \times 12 = 96$
$12 \times 8 = 96$
$12 \times 12 = 144$

There are only **9** new multiplications left in the book.

Every day of the week

The seven times table is useful for counting how many times things happen in a week, or over several weeks.

Count these in groups of seven

If you eat **5** fruits or vegetables a day, how many pieces is that a week?

If you wash your hands **6** times each day, how many times will you wash them in a week?

$5 \times 7 = 35$

If you brush your teeth twice a day, how many times is this a week?

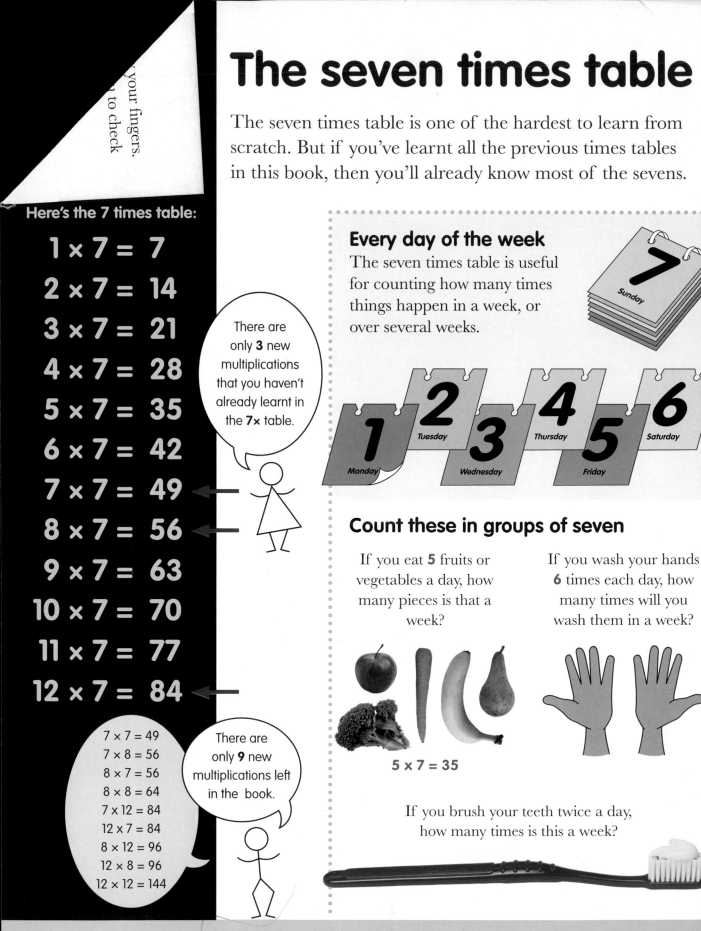

Fairytale division

The **7** dwarves have dug up these treasures in their mine, and want to share them out equally. Using division, can you work out how many each dwarf should receive?

They find **63** emeralds. How many does each dwarf get?

They find **35** gold nuggets. How many does each dwarf get?

They find **84** rubies. How many does each dwarf get?

63 ÷ 7 = 9

Odd ones out

Which of these are not multiples of **7**?

63

36

14

81

70

56

21

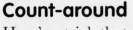

Count-around

Here's a trick that will help you remember **4 × 3** and **7 × 8**. If you follow the arrows around this sum, the numbers read " **1, 2, 3, 4.** "

$$4 \times 3 = 1\,2$$

The same thing works for **7 × 8**! Just think: " **5, 6, 7, 8.** "

$$8 \times 7 = 5\,6$$

There are seven stripes in a rainbow.

How many stripes are there in **7** rainbows?

What about **70** rainbows?

Or **700** rainbows?

Answers: 49 stripes, 490 stripes, 4,900 stripes.

Answers: 5 nuggets, 12 rubies. 36 and 81 are not multiples of 7.

43

7×

Patterns in the seven times table

Look at the pattern in this grid. These are the **first digits** for each answer (up to **9 × 7**) in the **7×** table.

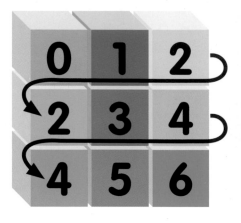

The number at the end of each is also the first number of the next line.

0, 1, 2 … 2, 3, 4 … 4, 5, 6

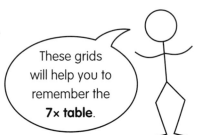

These grids will help you to remember the **7× table**.

Now try this one.

There's another special pattern in this grid. Start at the top right and read down, and you'll see the numbers **1** to **9**.

This grid gives the **final digits** for each answer (up to **9 × 7**) in the **7×** table.

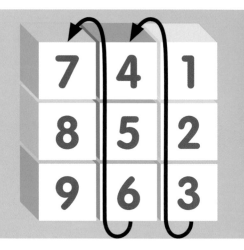

What happens if we put our two grids together?

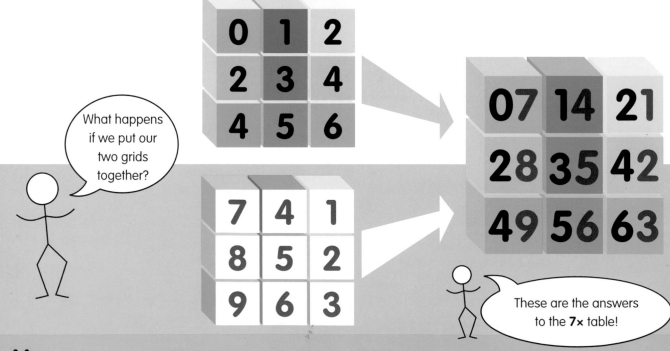

These are the answers to the **7×** table!

44

Gift boxes

You can find out the amount of space inside each of these boxes by multiplying together their length, height, and width. The answer will be in centimetres cubed (cm³).

3 cm × 2 cm ×

First, multiply **3** by

3 × 2 = 6

Multiply the answer by

6 × 7 = 42cm³

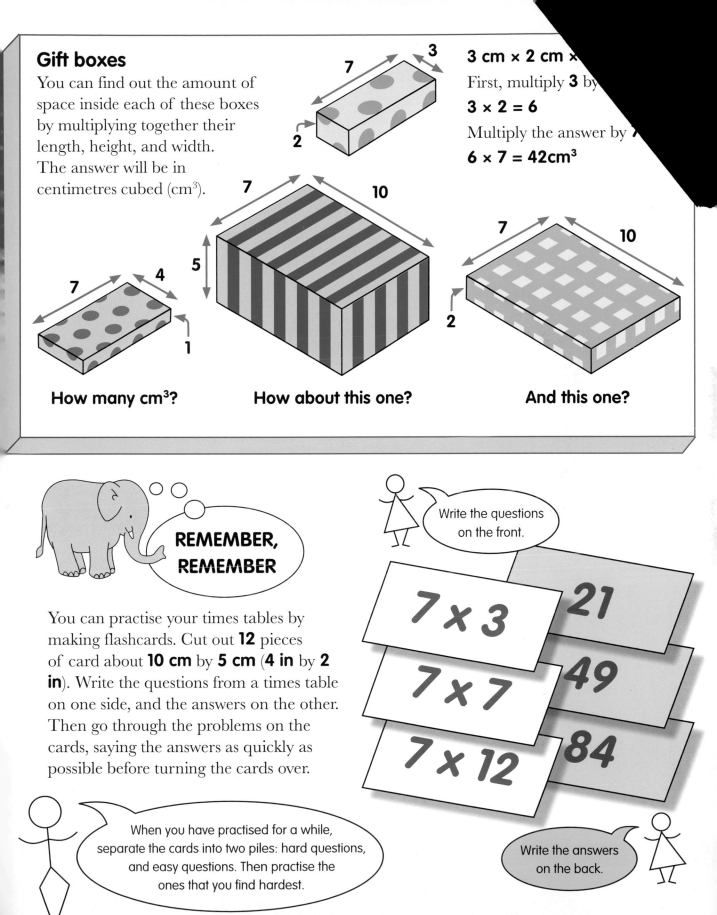

How many cm³?

How about this one?

And this one?

REMEMBER, REMEMBER

You can practise your times tables by making flashcards. Cut out **12** pieces of card about **10 cm** by **5 cm** (**4 in** by **2 in**). Write the questions from a times table on one side, and the answers on the other. Then go through the problems on the cards, saying the answers as quickly as possible before turning the cards over.

Write the questions on the front.

7 x 3   21

7 x 7   49

7 x 12   84

When you have practised for a while, separate the cards into two piles: hard questions, and easy questions. Then practise the ones that you find hardest.

Write the answers on the back.

The eight times table

There are several helpful patterns in the eight times table that will help you to learn it quickly.

Have you spotted the patterns?

Here's the 8 times table:

$1 \times 8 = 8$

$2 \times 8 = 16$

$3 \times 8 = 24$

$4 \times 8 = 32$

$5 \times 8 = 40$

$6 \times 8 = 48$

$7 \times 8 = 56$

$8 \times 8 = 64$

$9 \times 8 = 72$

$10 \times 8 = 80$

$11 \times 8 = 88$

$12 \times 8 = 96$

All the answers end in **even numbers.**

The units of the answers count down in **twos**.

8, 6, 4, 2, 0.
8, 6, 4, 2, 0.
Get the picture?

Counting in eights

Octopus arms and spider legs come in groups of eight. You can use the **8×** table to count them.

8 arms

8 legs

Count the arms and legs

How many arms on **4** octopuses?

$4 \times 8 = 32$

How many legs on **7** spiders?

How many arms on **9** octopuses?

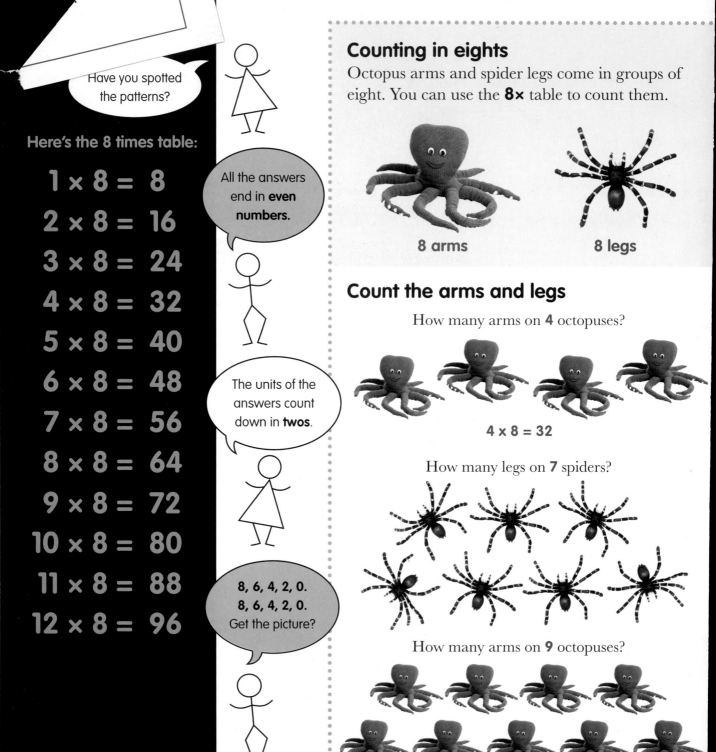

Answers: 56 spider legs, 72 octopus arms.

Game of chess

The **2** players in a game of chess each have **2** rows of **8** pieces. How many pieces are there altogether?

A chessboard has **8 × 8** squares. How many squares are there in total?

Odd ones out

Which of these numbers are not multiples of **8**?

56 24 74

14 32

93 44 64

TOP TIP

If you can't remember a multiplication in the eight times table, remember that the answers in the eight times table are double the answers in the four times table.

6 × 4 = 24

And **24 × 2 = 48**

So **6 × 8 = 48**

Times tables tennis

You have to think fast in this two-player game.

1. First decide which times table you're going to practise (for example the **8×** table). Then decide which player is going to "serve", and which one will "return".

2. The server calls out numbers between one and twelve. The returning player must call back the answer to that number multiplied by **8** (or whichever times table you've chosen).

3. As soon as the returning player hesitates or gets an answer wrong, the players swap round, and the returning player starts to serve.

5! 40! 3! 24!

Answers: 32 chess pieces, and 64 squares. 74, 14, 93, and 44 are not multiples of 8.

47

Division with remainders

When you can't divide a number equally, some will be left over. This leftover portion is called a remainder. To divide **19** by **8**, count down from **19** until you find a number that is in the **8** times table.

16 is the nearest multiple of **8**.

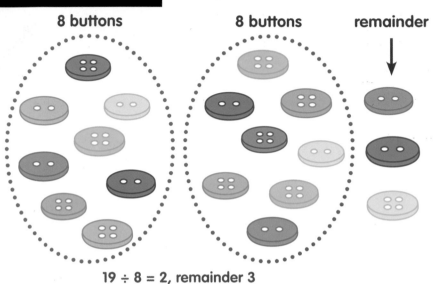

8 buttons **8 buttons** remainder

19, 18, 17, 16...

How many times does **8** go into **16**?

The answer is 2.

How many are left over as a remainder?

19 − 16 = 3

19 ÷ 8 = 2, remainder 3

What is the answer to **25 ÷ 8**?

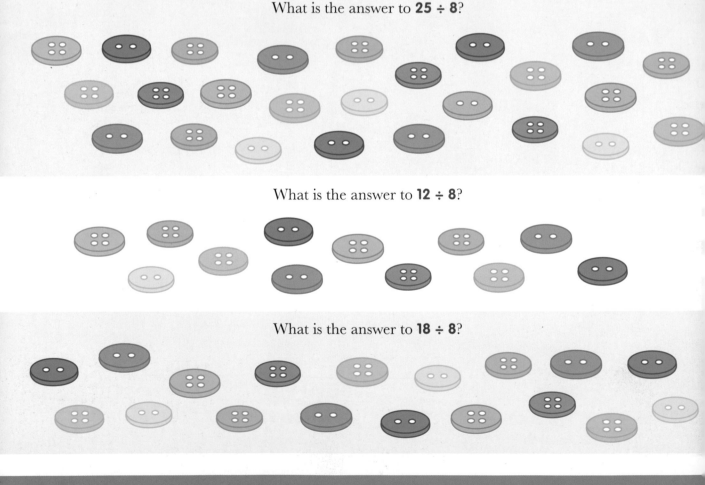

What is the answer to **12 ÷ 8**?

What is the answer to **18 ÷ 8**?

Monkey puzzle

There are **8** monkeys in the zoo's monkey enclosure, and the keeper has some crates full of different kinds of fruit. She wants to give each monkey the same amount of fruit, and this will mean that some fruit is left in each crate.

How many apples can each monkey have if there are **26** apples in all? How many will be left over?

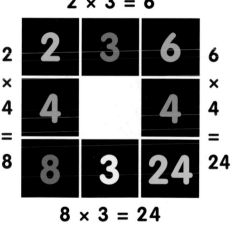

How many oranges can each monkey have if there are **76** oranges altogether? How many will be left over?

How many bananas can each monkey have if there are **41** bananas altogether? How many will be left over?

Puzzle squares

Copy these puzzle squares onto a blank piece of paper. Can you work out which numbers are missing from each square? The first two numbers in each row or column must multiply together to give the last number in that row or column.

2 × 3 = 6

	2	3	6	6
2				
×	4		4	×
4				4
=				=
8	8	3	24	24

8 × 3 = 24

Fill in the missing squares. (Solution on page 64.)

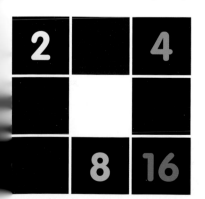

2		4
	8	16

2		8
	4	48

TOP TIP

Dividing by **8** can be tricky. It's much easier to halve a number. If you ever get stuck, instead of dividing by **8**, try halving, halving and halving again.

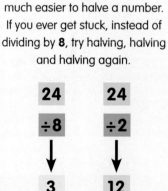

| 24 |
| ÷8 |
| ↓ |
| 3 |

| 24 |
| ÷2 |
| ↓ |
| 12 |
| ÷2 |
| ↓ |
| 6 |
| ÷2 |
| ↓ |
| 3 |

It works the other way round, too: you can multiply by **8** by doubling three times.

Answers: 9 oranges (4 left over), 3 apples (2 left over), 5 bananas (1 left over).

49

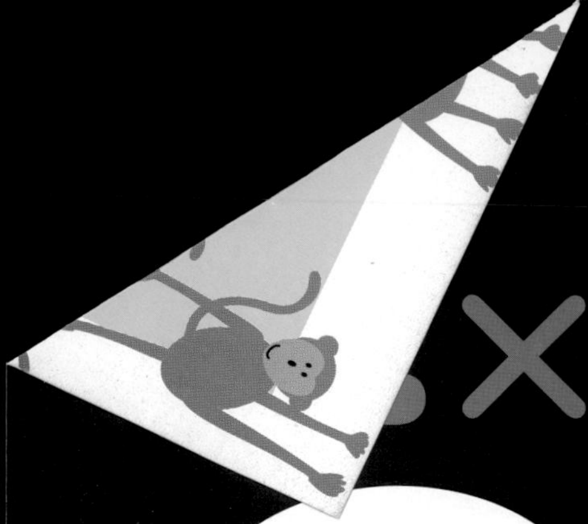

The twelve times table

This is the last times table to learn – or do you know it already? We've already covered **143** of the **144** equations from the **1** to **12** times tables, so now there should only be one equation you don't know.

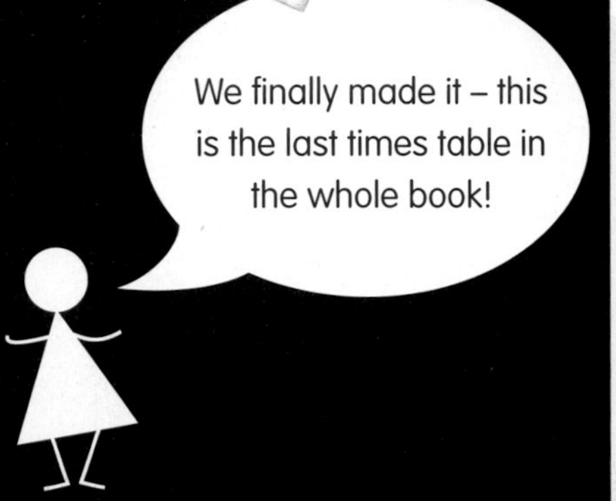

We finally made it – this is the last times table in the whole book!

Here's the 12 times table:

$1 \times 12 = 12$

$2 \times 12 = 24$

$3 \times 12 = 36$

$4 \times 12 = 48$

$5 \times 12 = 60$

$6 \times 12 = 72$

$7 \times 12 = 84$

$8 \times 12 = 96$

$9 \times 12 = 108$

$10 \times 12 = 120$

$11 \times 12 = 132$

$12 \times 12 = 144$

The 12× table – fast

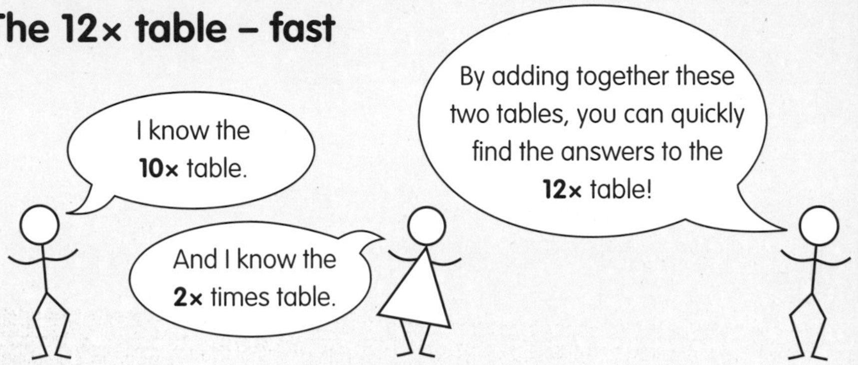

I know the **10×** table.
And I know the **2×** times table.
By adding together these two tables, you can quickly find the answers to the **12×** table!

How many candles on these **5** birthday cakes?

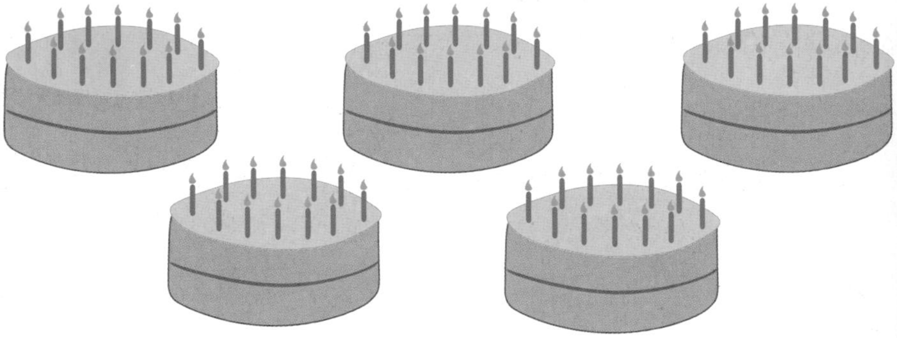

How many hearts are on these **3** wedding cakes?

How many coloured sweets on these **4** chocolate cakes?

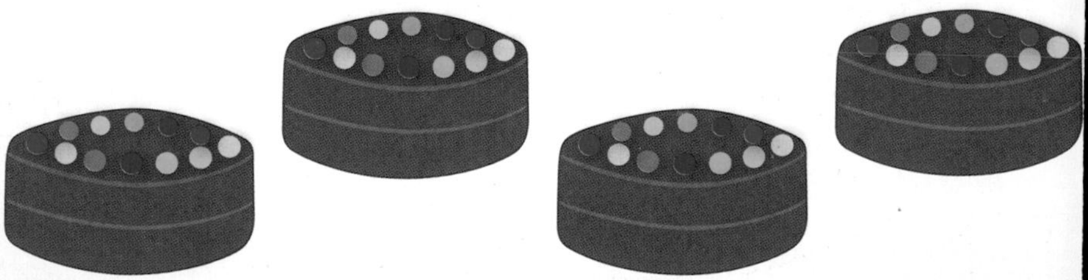

Answers: 60 candles, 36 hearts, 48 coloured sweets.

Record-breaking dice game

Now that you have learnt the times tables up to **12 × 12**, you can play a simple game to revise them. Roll two dice, and make a mental note of the number you scored. Roll the dice again, and multiply the first number by the second. Did you get it right? Check your answer. See how many you can get right in a row – then try to beat your own record!

Quick-thinking dice game

Here's another dice game you can play with a friend. Roll two dice, then roll them again. You must multiply the first number you got by the second. Whoever calls out the right answer first scores a point. Keep playing until one player wins by scoring **10** points.

REMEMBER, REMEMBER

These are the hardest equations in the **12×** table:

11 × 12 = 132   **12 × 12 = 144**

Write each of these on a flash card. Then fix the cards to each side of your bedroom door, using sticky tack. Before you can open the door you must give the password – which is the answer on the back of the card.

Tied together

Which of these equations have the same answers? Untangle the strings to find out if you're right.

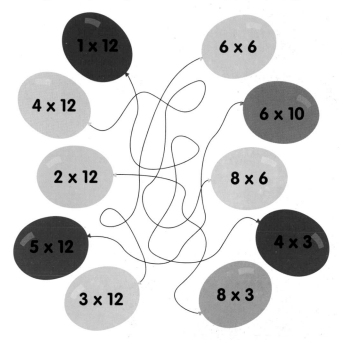

1 × 12   6 × 6   4 × 12   6 × 10   2 × 12   8 × 6   5 × 12   4 × 3   3 × 12   8 × 3

Whack-a-mole

If you bop a mole on the head, you score **12** times the number on its card. How many points is each mole worth? See if you can answer them all in less than **30** seconds.

5   1   7
8   11   3
12   4   10
2   9   6

Answers: Moles, left to right and top to bottom: 60, 12, 84, 96, 132, 36, 144, 48, 120, 24, 108, 72.

51

12×

Odd ones out

Which of these numbers are not multiples of **12**?

108 60 70 144

54 142 24

Number cards are worth **2–10** points.
Jacks count as **11** points.
Queens count as **12** points.
Kings count as **12** points.

The ace is worth **1** point.

Times tables snap

This is a game for two players. You'll need a pack of cards with the jokers taken out.

1) Shuffle the pack and deal the cards face down between the players. They should each have a pile of **26** cards in front of them.

2) Both players flip over the card on the top of their deck. Whoever calls out the correct product first wins both cards. (The product is the answer to those two cards multiplied together.) They put the cards they've won in a separate winnings pile.

3) If one of the players calls out the wrong answer, the other player wins both cards.

4) If both players call out the correct answer at the same time, that round is a draw, and the players must turn over more cards until there is a clear winner. All the cards turned over then go to the winner of that round.

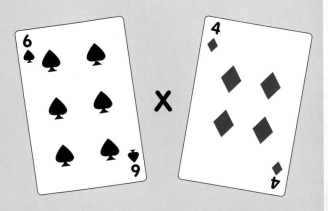

6 × 4 = 24
I win!

And the winner is...

The player with the most cards in their winnings pile at the end of the game has won.

Times tables bingo

You can play this game with two or more friends – the more people, the better. One person has to be the caller, and the other people are the players.

1) First, each player needs to draw a grid of **25** squares on a piece of paper, like this (see right).

2) Then they write a number in each square. They can choose any numbers from the list below. The caller and other players mustn't look at what they are writing.

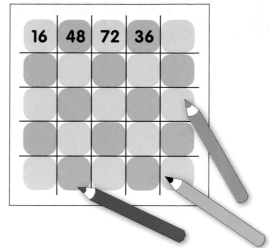

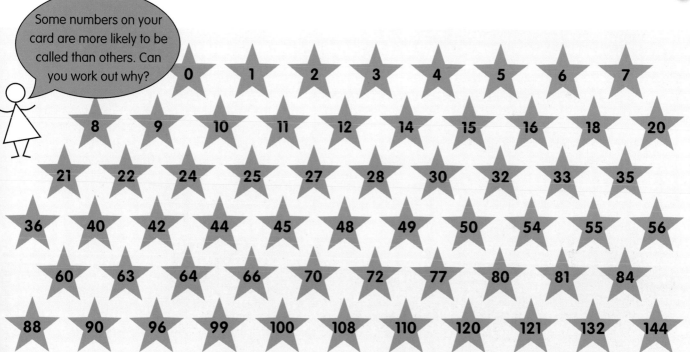

Some numbers on your card are more likely to be called than others. Can you work out why?

0 1 2 3 4 5 6 7

8 9 10 11 12 14 15 16 18 20

21 22 24 25 27 28 30 32 33 35

36 40 42 44 45 48 49 50 54 55 56

60 63 64 66 70 72 77 80 81 84

88 90 96 99 100 108 110 120 121 132 144

3) When the players have written down all their numbers, the caller starts to shout out problems from the **0** to **12** times tables. If a player has the answer to one of the equations on their sheet, they should cross it out.

And the winner is...
The first person to cross out all the answers on their sheet should shout out "BINGO!"

Bingo!

Count on me
Did you know it's possible to count from **1** to **12** on one hand? Touch the tip of your thumb to each of the joints of your fingers in turn.

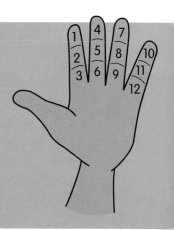

How well do you know your times tables?

You can test yourself on all the tables up to **12×** with the puzzles here. Make a note of any problems you find especially difficult – that way you can practise them later. The answers are on page 64.

How many legs?

| 12 spiders | 7 elephants | 5 ladybirds | 9 ducks | 11 snakes |

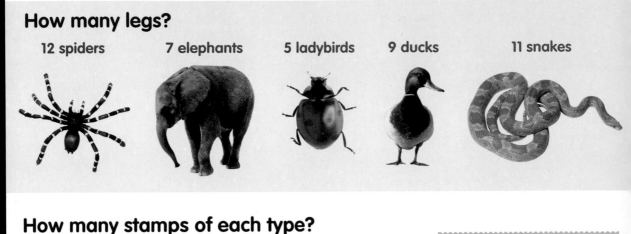

How many stamps of each type?

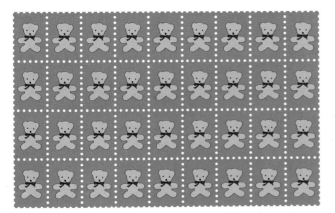

Dominoes

Multiply the two halves of these dominoes together.

At the toy shop

You have **£4.68** in your piggy bank. How many of each of these could you afford? How much would be left as a remainder?

£1.17   90p   50p   £2.30

Pizza party

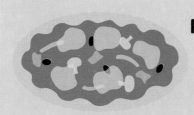

You're making some pizzas for your friends and family. If you're dividing the toppings equally between the pizzas, how many of these toppings will you put on each pizza?

54 slices of green pepper between **6** pizzas

18 olives between **3** pizzas

55 pieces of pepperoni between **5** pizzas

42 slices of mushroom between **6** pizzas

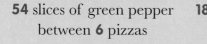
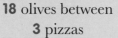

Puzzle grid

Copy this grid onto a blank piece of paper. In each box, write the answer to the numbers along the top multiplied by the numbers along the side.

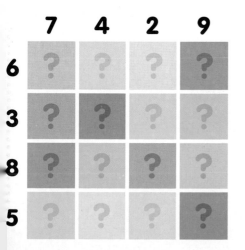

	7	4	2	9
6	?	?	?	?
3	?	?	?	?
8	?	?	?	?
5	?	?	?	?

Helping around the house

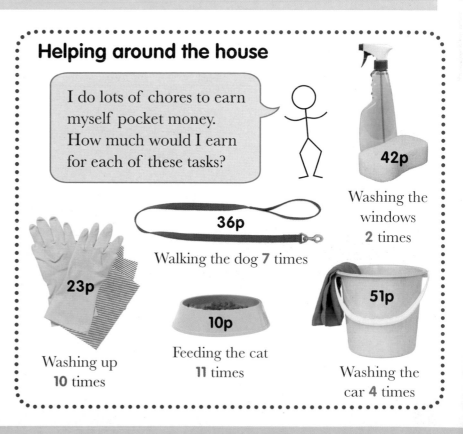

I do lots of chores to earn myself pocket money. How much would I earn for each of these tasks?

42p
Washing the windows **2** times

36p
Walking the dog **7** times

23p
Washing up **10** times

10p
Feeding the cat **11** times

51p
Washing the car **4** times

Long multiplication

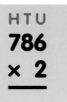

Don't you touch that calculator!

Multiplying a large number by a single-digit number

This isn't as hard as it looks, but you will need to know your times tables up to **10 × 10** pretty well before you try this.

Write the large number above the small one.

```
H T U
786
× 2
```

Multiply the single-digit number on the bottom by the units, then tens, then hundreds of the number at the top.

```
786     Multiply by units
×  2
  12  →  6 × 2 = 12
```

```
786     Multiply by tens
×  2
  12
 160  →  80 × 2 = 160
```

```
786     Multiply by hundreds
×  2
  12
 160
1400  →  700 × 2 = 1,400
```

```
   12   Finally, add up the
  160   answers to those
+1400   three multiplications.
────
 1572   So: 786 × 2 = 1,572
```

Now let's try the fast way

A quicker way of doing this is to write the answer to each multiplication on the same line, going from right to left. If you get an answer of ten or more when you're multiplying the units, tens, or hundreds, you "carry" the first digit of that answer, adding it to the column to the left.

```
285
×  3    5 × 3 = 15
────
   5
────
 1      Carry 1 to tens column.
```

```
285    8 × 3 = 24
×  3
────
  55   24 + 1 = 25
────
2 1    Carry 2 to hundreds column.
```

```
285    2 × 3 = 6
×  3
────
855    6 + 2 = 8
────
2 1
```

Now have a go

```
385     723     210     974
×  2    ×  4    ×  3    ×  8
```

Multiplying two large numbers together

If you are multiplying together two numbers that have more than one digit, things get a little trickier. Keep practising and you'll soon pick it up.

First concentrate on the unit digit at the bottom, and multiply it by each number on the top row in turn.

H T U
824 Ignore this 3 at first.
× 36 Multiply 6 by 4, then 2, then 8.

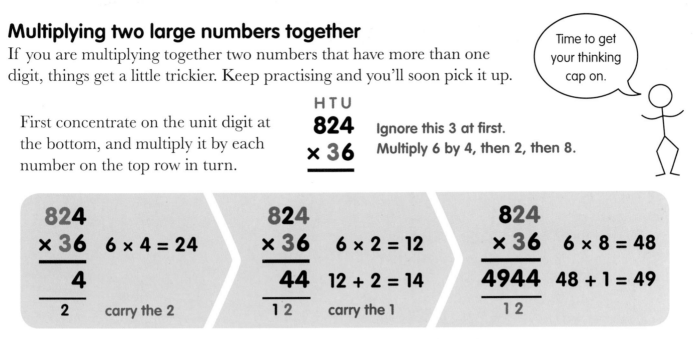

824
× 36   6 × 4 = 24
4
2   carry the 2

824
× 36   6 × 2 = 12
44   12 + 2 = 14
1 2   carry the 1

824
× 36   6 × 8 = 48
4944   48 + 1 = 49
1 2

Now look at the tens digit at the bottom, and multiply it by the units, tens and hundreds digits in the top row. But first you need to add a zero, because you're multiplying by numbers in the tens column.

824
× 36   3 × 4 = 12
4944
20   Add a zero
1   carry the 1

824
× 36   3 × 2 = 6
4944   6 + 1 = 7
720
1

824
× 36   3 × 8 = 24
4944
24720
1

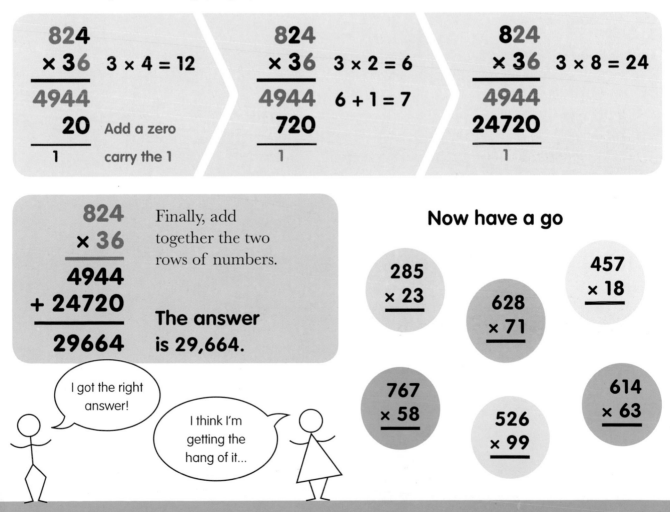

824
× 36
4944
+ 24720
29664

Finally, add together the two rows of numbers.

The answer is 29,664.

I got the right answer!

I think I'm getting the hang of it...

Now have a go

285
× 23

628
× 71

457
× 18

767
× 58

526
× 99

614
× 63

Answers: Blue – 6,555. Purple – 44,588. Yellow – 44,486. Red – 8,226. Green – 52,074. Pink – 38,682.

57

Window-frame multiplication

Here's another way of multiplying large numbers together.
Some people find this easier than standard long multiplication.

Say, for example, you want to multiply 45 by 6.
A) The number **45** has **2** digits, so draw **2** rectangular boxes side by side.
B) Draw a diagonal line across each box, from the bottom left-hand corner to the top right-hand corner.
C) Write the numbers you want to multiply along the top and right-hand side of the boxes.

The number **6** is only one digit long, so only one row of boxes is needed.

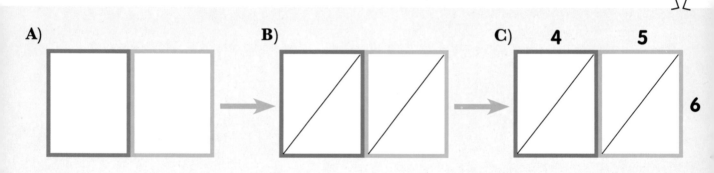

D) Multiply the digits along the top and side, starting from the right.
5 × 6 = 30, so write **3** and **0** on either side of the diagonal line.
E) Now do the multiplication in the next box along. **4 × 6 = 24**, so write **2** and **4**.
F) Look at the numbers in each diagonal column. These give you the answer to **45 × 6**. If there are two numbers in a diagonal column, add them together.

Add together the numbers in the purple column.

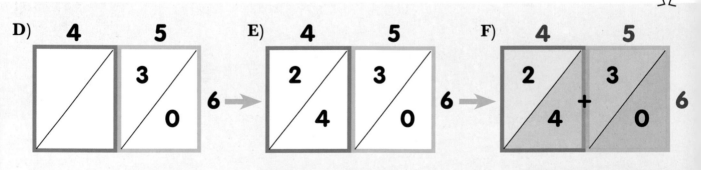

45 × 6 = 270

Window-frame multiplication works for larger numbers, too. Read the answers down the left-hand side and across the bottom of the boxes.

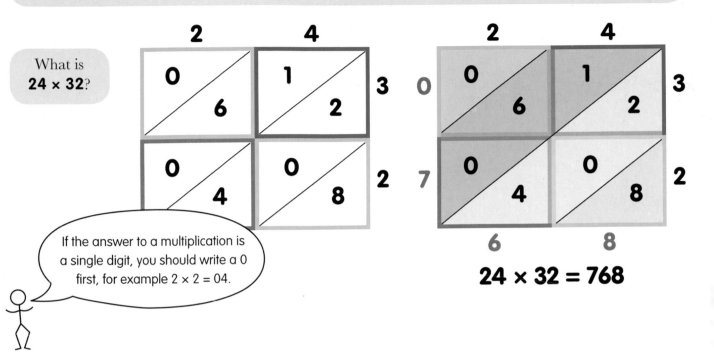

What is
24 × 32?

If the answer to a multiplication is a single digit, you should write a 0 first, for example 2 × 2 = 04.

24 × 32 = 768

If a diagonal column adds up to a two-digit answer, you should carry the first digit, adding it to the number on the left.

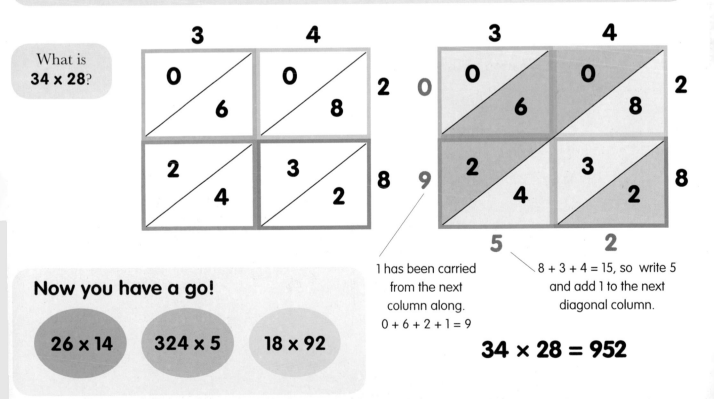

What is
34 × 28?

1 has been carried from the next column along.
0 + 6 + 2 + 1 = 9

8 + 3 + 4 = 15, so write 5 and add 1 to the next diagonal column.

34 × 28 = 952

Now you have a go!

26 × 14   324 × 5   18 × 92

Long division

No calculators allowed!

Division is something that we use all the time, and you won't always have a calculator to hand. So it's worth learning how to divide large numbers with just a pen and paper.

Short division

Short division means dividing a large number by a one-digit number.

This isn't as hard as I thought.

Write **651 ÷ 3** like this:

$$3\overline{)651}$$

1) Divide each digit of the large number by the one-digit number, from left to right.
2) If you get a remainder, put this in front of the next digit along.

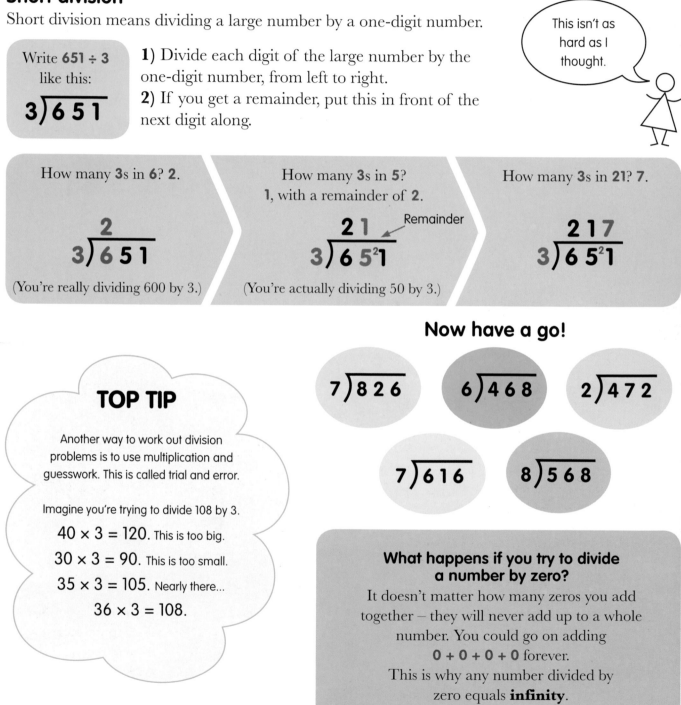

How many **3**s in **6**? **2**.

$$3\overline{)6\overset{2}{}51}$$

(You're really dividing 600 by 3.)

How many **3**s in **5**?
1, with a remainder of **2**.

$$3\overline{)6\,5^2 1}$$ ← Remainder

(You're actually dividing 50 by 3.)

How many **3**s in **21**? **7**.

$$3\overline{)6\,5^2 1}$$ → 217

Now have a go!

$$7\overline{)826}$$ $$6\overline{)468}$$ $$2\overline{)472}$$

$$7\overline{)616}$$ $$8\overline{)568}$$

TOP TIP

Another way to work out division problems is to use multiplication and guesswork. This is called trial and error.

Imagine you're trying to divide 108 by 3.

$40 \times 3 = 120$. This is too big.

$30 \times 3 = 90$. This is too small.

$35 \times 3 = 105$. Nearly there...

$36 \times 3 = 108$.

What happens if you try to divide a number by zero?

It doesn't matter how many zeros you add together – they will never add up to a whole number. You could go on adding
0 + 0 + 0 + 0 forever.
This is why any number divided by zero equals **infinity**.

Long division

This is a bit trickier. Make sure your brain is in gear before you tackle these problems!

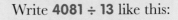

Write **4081 ÷ 13** like this:

$$13\overline{)4081}$$

Now have a go!

How many times does **13** go into **4**? None, so move along one digit.

$$13\overline{)4081}$$

Work from left to right.

How many times does **13** go into **40**? **3** times – so put a **3** above the **0**.

3 times **13** is only **39**. So we subtract **39** from **40** to get the remainder: **1**.

$$
\begin{array}{r}
3 \\
13\overline{)4081} \\
-39 \\
\hline
1
\end{array}
$$

13 goes into 40 3 times.

3 × 13 = 39

Remainder

$$36\overline{)845}$$

$$24\overline{)5361}$$

Now you need to deal with the **8**. Move it down alongside the **1**, to make **18**.

How many times does **13** go into **18**? **1** time – so put a **1** above the **8**.

1 times **13** is **13**. Subtract this from **18** to find the remainder – **5**.

$$
\begin{array}{r}
31 \\
13\overline{)4081} \\
-39\downarrow \\
\hline
18 \\
-13 \\
\hline
5
\end{array}
$$

13 goes into 18 once.

1 × 13 = 13

Remainder

$$13\overline{)823}$$

$$23\overline{)4810}$$

Move the **1** down.

How many times does **13** go into **51**? **3** times, with a remainder of **12**.

There are no more digits to carry down, so we're finished. Phew.

The answer is **313**, remainder **12**.

$$
\begin{array}{r}
313 \\
13\overline{)4081} \\
39 \\
\hline
18 \\
-13 \\
\hline
51 \\
39 \\
\hline
12
\end{array}
$$

13 goes into 51 3 times.

3 × 13 = 39

Final remainder

I think I need a break now!

Answers: 23, remainder 17. 223, remainder 9. 63, remainder 3. 209, remainder 4. 23, remainder 3.

61

Times tables grid

Use this grid to check your answers.

To find the product of a multiplication, simply trace your fingers along the row and column matching each of the numbers you want to multiply together, until you find the point where they meet.

✕	1	2	3	4	5	6	7	8	9	10	11	12
1	1	2	3	4	5	6	7	8	9	10	11	12
2	2	4	6	8	10	12	14	16	18	20	22	24
3	3	6	9	12	15	18	21	24	27	30	33	36
4	4	8	12	16	20	24	28	32	36	40	44	48
5	5	10	15	20	25	30	35	40	45	50	55	60
6	6	12	18	24	30	36	42	48	54	60	66	72
7	7	14	21	28	35	42	49	56	63	70	77	84
8	8	16	24	32	40	48	56	64	72	80	88	96
9	9	18	27	36	45	54	63	72	81	90	99	108
10	10	20	30	40	50	60	70	80	90	100	110	120
11	11	22	33	44	55	66	77	88	99	110	121	132
12	12	24	36	48	60	72	84	96	108	120	132	144

This line is called the leading diagonal. The answers on either side of the line are mirror images of each other.

Glossary

Here are some important times tables words and phrases.

Don't get stuck – look it up!

Area how we measure the size of a surface. Area is measured in square units, for example, square metres.

Carry move a digit from one column to another in an addition or multiplication equation.

Difference what is left after one number is taken away from another.

Digits the symbols that make up numbers. For example, **25** is made up of the digits **2** and **5**.

Dividend a number that is divided by another in a division equation.

Division splitting a number into equal parts. One example of division is sharing between people. Division is the opposite of multiplication.

Divisible can be divided into a whole number, without a remainder. For example, **8** is divisible by **4**, because **8 ÷ 4 = 2**, and **2** is a whole number.

Divisor a number by which another number is divided. In the equation **20 ÷ 5 = 4**, **5** is the divisor.

Even number a whole number that can be divided by **2** without a remainder. Even numbers end with the digits **0**, **2**, **4**, **6**, or **8**.

Factor whole numbers that can be multiplied together to make another number. For example **3** and **6** are factors of **18**.

Multiple a number that can be divided by another number without a remainder. For example, **54** is a multiple of **6** because **9 × 6 = 54**.

Multiplication adding the same number over and over again.

Multiplier a number that is multiplied by another number.

Odd number a whole number that cannot be divided by **2** without a remainder. Odd numbers end with the digits **1**, **3**, **5**, **7**, or **9**.

Prime number a number that only has two factors: **1** and itself.

Product the result of a multiplication. In the equation **3 × 5 = 15**, **15** is the product.

Remainder when you have divided a whole number into smaller whole numbers, what is left over is called the remainder.

Units the last digit in a whole number. For example, in **513** the unit is **3**.

Volume a measurement of how much a three-dimensional shape could contain, measured in units cubed, for example, metres cubed.

Whole number a number that does not end in a decimal or fraction.

Thank you for reading!

BYE BYE!

Acknowledgments: Thank you to Wendy Horobin, Alexander Cox, and Lorrie Mack for editorial assistance.
Picture credits: The publisher would like to thank the following for their kind permission to reproduce their photographs:
(Key: a-above; b-below/bottom; c-centre; f-far; l-left; r-right; t-top)
DK Images: Jane Bull 2cla, 30crb; Indianapolis Motor Speedway Foundation Inc. 4br; Lorraine Electronics Surveillance 26fbl, 31c; Natural History Museum, London 43cl; Stephen Oliver 7ca, 55ftr. **Getty Images:** Stone / Catherine Ledner 5cr. **iStockphoto.com:** Avava 5tl; bluestocking 4cb, 4clb, 4crb, 4fclb, 4fcrb; Joel Carillet 5tc; Angelo Gilardelli 52cla; Lasavinaproduccions 39bl, 39cl, 39cla, 39clb; Vasko Miokovic 5tr; Skip ODonnell 5c, 47cr; Denis Sarbashev 43tl; James Steidl 7cl, 7fcl; Ivonne Wierink-vanWetten 49tl.
All other images © Dorling Kindersley. For further information see: www.dkimages.com

Answers

Times tables quiz
Pages 32–33

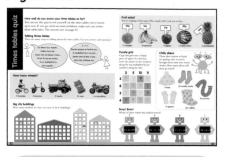

Talking times tables

$6 \times 4 = 24$	$5 \times 7 = 35$
$12 \times 10 = 120$	$11 \times 12 = 132$
$7 \times 11 = 77$	$5 \times 0 = 0$
$3 \times 10 = 30$	$7 \times 4 = 28$
$4 \times 2 = 8$	$9 \times 3 = 27$

How many wheels?
22 wheels on 11 bicycles
12 wheels on 4 tricycles
20 wheels on 5 trucks
48 wheels on 12 cars
12 wheels on 6 motorbikes

Big city buildings
30 windows in the purple building,
red building – 32, yellow building – 21,
green building – 25

Fruit salad
£1.00 for 4 oranges
96p for 6 bananas
£3.41 for 11 apples
82p for 1 watermelon
£1.26 for 2 pineapples

Puzzle grid

6	15	30	33
16	40	80	88
10	25	50	55
8	20	40	44

Chilly aliens
There are enough hats for 4 aliens.
7 aliens can wear gloves.
9 aliens can wear scarves.
7 aliens can wear woolly socks.
12 aliens can wear wellies.

Error! Error!
The green robot
has malfunctioned.

He should have
said: $28 \div 4 = 7$.

Times tables quiz
Pages 54–55

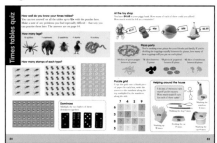

How many legs?
12 spiders have 96 legs.
7 elephants have 28 legs.
5 ladybirds have 30 legs.
9 ducks have 18 legs.
11 snakes have 0 legs.

How many stamps of each type?
15 fish stamps
36 car stamps
32 flower stamps
36 teddy bear stamps

Dominoes

$3 \times 1 = 3$	$5 \times 3 = 15$
$6 \times 4 = 24$	$2 \times 6 = 12$

At the toy shop
4 dolls (no remainder)
5 toy cars (18p remainder)
9 beach balls (18p remainder)
2 toy boats (8p remainder)

Pizza party
9 pieces of pepper, 6 olives,
11 pieces of pepperoni,
7 pieces of mushroom

Puzzle grid

42	24	12	54
21	12	6	27
56	32	16	72
35	20	10	45

Helping around the house
£2.30 for washing up
£2.52 for walking the dog
£1.10 for feeding the cat
£2.04 for washing the car
84p for washing the windows

8x table squares
Page 49

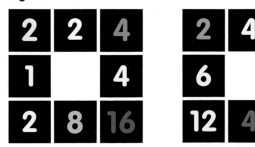

3x table minefield
Page 30

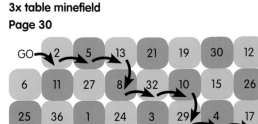